FREEDOM FROM SUBSTANCES

Ending addiction through the Gospel

by Douglas Clarke

BookSpecs Publishing
Pennsville, New Jersey

FREEDOM FROM SUBSTANCES
Ending addiction through the Gospel
Copyright © 2018
Douglas Clarke

ISBN 9781724149626

Published by BookSpecs Publishing
16 Sunset Ave., Pennsville, NJ 08070

For More Information, visit:
www.FaithWithReason.com

What others are saying about this book:

"Doug Clarke's "Freedom from Substances" is a book about hope in that through Doug's use of experiential language with the support of applicable scripture, God will open the eyes of the reader in such a way that they will understand the grace of God in the face of their addiction."
- Ralph Menichini Managing Director of 2nd Timothy 3:16 Ministries

"Douglas calculates that as an addict, he broke the Law of God 43,800 times rendering him guilty as hell before God. Instead of offering a "three step solution" that could never atone for or reverse 43,800 infractions of the Law of God, Doug offers the Gospel. A simple Story. Douglas Clarke, a man who has been to hell and back, a man who has many degrees and accompaniments behind his name, offers "Nothing But Jesus" as a remedy to hard addiction. Let that sink in as you read this book."
Rev., Dr. Chuck L. Betters, Senior Pastor, Reach Church, Chairman, Reach Christian Schools, Inc.

"Douglas Clarke offers a hard-hitting, thought-provoking book on addiction that begins with his personal journey and ends with Christ's redemptive work on the cross. Are you suffering under the slavery of addiction? Are you searching for hope? Do you know someone who is in desperate need of help? Doug takes the reader into the depths of his own struggle with addiction – but he doesn't leave you there. Instead, he

points to the freedom and forgiveness found in Jesus Christ! Highly recommended!"

- Joseph A. Vangeli, Chief Program Officer, Jubilee Ministries

This book is dedicated to Lindsay Clarke, my best friend, companion, and heart who has supported and loved me through the journey that the Lord has taken us on.

To the men I have ministered to at Jubilee Ministries, Hoffman Hall, and Luzerne Treatment Center ... Never forget ... Our salvation is found in the person and work of Jesus Christ alone.

Acknowledgements

First and foremost, I must honor and give credit to my father, Ronald W. Clarke. You have shown me what it means to follow Christ and have provided me an example of what a godly man looks like. I pray that the Lord allows me to be half the man you are. I thank my mother, Pamela Clarke for believing in the work that Christ is doing in my life. Your encouragement and zeal for the Lord has empowered me to preach the Gospel to those who are sick and hurting. To my wonderful children: Anthony, Chloe, and Zeke, you are the reason that I push forward in my spiritual walk in the hope that someday Christ may form in you through seeing Christ formed in me.

To those who have invested in and ministered to me as the Lord has taken me on this journey. To my friend and beloved brother Joseph Cain, I thank you for the way that you invested in my family and believed that the Lord was calling me to Pastoral ministry. To the pastoral staff at Reach Church, I praise God for your faithfulness in preaching the message of "Nothing but Jesus." You will never know how this message has impacted my life. To my mentor and friend Joe Vangeli, your godly leadership has taught me to exemplify Christ in and out of ministry. I am grateful to you for giving me an opportunity to minister to the men at Jubilee. To my uncle, mentor, and fellow worker according to the grace given to us, Ralph Menichini, you will never know the profound impact that you have had on my spiritual walk and ministry endeavors. I am forever grateful to you for teaching me early in my faith that God's plan of redemption begins before time began and that there is nothing I can do to save myself.

Finally, to my wife, Lindsay, this journey is not possible without you. Through the trials and tribulations we have faced over the past few years, you have stood firm. You have fought alongside me and have gone with me in every direction that we felt the Lord was calling us. You have held me up when I was weak and encouraged me through it all. This book, ministry, and story don't exist apart from your love and support.

Contents

Introduction

---◆---

Here I Am Now

As I sit here examining where I currently am, I'm amazed at everything that has happened in my personal and professional life. It is so strange to sit and speak of all the wonderful things that I have seen take place, the things that I have accomplished, and the joy that I currently feel. How strange it is to kiss my children goodnight and feel confident as their father. To wake up every day and be a productive member of society is a paradox when applied to a person like me.

Equally as astounding is the professional quest that I have embarked on over the past five years. Just last year, I held the position of Director a 120-bed residential re-entry program and the position of Operations Manager of a 100-bed drug and alcohol treatment center in the city of Philadelphia, both of which were contracted through the Pennsylvania Department of Corrections, Department of Drug and Alcohol Programs, and the Pennsylvania Board of Probation and Parole. As bizarre as it may seem, I left this career in treatment in pursuit of servanthood in the field of full time ministry. As of today, I am the Aftercare Manager of a Christian residential re-entry program that helps those who have struggled with addiction and incarceration.

Beyond my profession endeavors, in May of 2017, I was awarded my bachelor's degree in science with a major in Religion. At the time of writing this book, I am coming to a close on my pursuit of a master's degree in theological studies. I view both degrees as mere stepping stones in my pursuit of a doctorate in philosophy. Nearly all the accomplishments I have listed were once mere goals that have now become realities. Hopefully, the future ambitions that I now hold will manifest as well. But as I reflect on all of this it amazes me because I realize now that I accomplished absolutely none of it on my own power.

Just the very thought of these accomplishments and dreams overwhelms me. This is partly due to the fact that who I am today is not who I was just a few short years ago. The professional I am today, the student I am today, the father I am today, the husband I am today, this person at one point in time didn't exist. And the only professional accomplishment I ever previously had was being a professional junkie. My area of expertise was opioid abuse, and my only aspirations were the next day's fix.

The idea of the man I am today was once a fantasy that was suffocated by the reality of my drug abuse. Though I would often dream of being the man I am today, all efforts towards becoming this person were strangled out of me as dope sickness set in and hope drifted away. All of my efforts and all of my trying were unsuccessful. What is interesting is it seems that the harder I worked to do good the harder I fell into drug abuse, and the deeper the pit of my addiction became. How strange it is that just a mere six years ago, I sat at the bottom of my pit, completely consumed by sorrow, fear, and enslavement to heroin.

This is why it is so surreal to reflect on the current life that I live. As I sit writing this, my children are tucked safely into their beds, my wife is asleep in bed, and I sit contently pondering my existence – just as I used to when I was in the grip of my addiction. As I sit and ponder my past, present and future, who I once was and who I am now, I am humbled by the answer to one simple question, *"How did I get here?"* However, before this question can be answered, there must be an understanding of where I came from.

1

A Slave to My Addiction

Prior to becoming the person I am now – prior to coming fact-to-face with Jesus – I was a professional drug addict. I knew nothing but drugs. I could do nothing but get high. I was defined by my persistent drug abuse. The next day's fix was the all-consuming fire that burned within the depths of my soul. I began to take pride in my ability to radically push my body's limits of abuse and escape the ever present hand of death. I would often embark on death defying journeys through experimentation with various narcotic cocktails, each of which ultimately led to the fearful thought, "*This may be the time that kills me*." Looking back now, I am amazed at the fact that I am writing this – and that I am not dead.

Along with my ever-present pursuit of the high, I also was addicted to the lifestyle that came with it. The pursuit of that lifestyle brought with it a slew of horrors that molded and shaped me into a monster. My lifestyle became consumed by darkness and defined by crime, lying, cheating, stealing, and sexual promiscuity. As I sunk deeper into the depths of addiction, these acts attached themselves to my character and began to define who I was as a human being. The vile acts I committed and pursued maintained my addiction. My addiction defined who I was. Outside of addiction I knew nothing, and I could do nothing else. But inside my addiction I was a master at my craft.

I would sadly often dream about and desire the life I have now. I'd think about having a home with a white picket fence. I'd think about having a loving wife and children and a pet dog. I longed for a life where I didn't have to stress about where the next high was coming from, let alone the next dollar. I was physically, mentally, and spiritually hardwired to be an addict and had no idea how this could be undone.

The best picture to describe how addiction consumed my hopes and dreams may seem somewhat silly or immature, but the movie *Major Payne* is the only way to describe my dilemma. Major Payne was a comedy about a trained military killer who only knew war, yet at the completion of his final tour he was assigned to run an ROTC program at a prep school. In the end Major Payne falls in love with a beautiful teacher, adopts one of the boys, and lives happily ever after.

In one particular scene, Major Payne has been called back to war and he chooses to leave behind the beautiful teacher, leave his boys, and leave behind his new life. As he sits waiting for his train, he looks beyond the tracks before him and begins to envision life beyond war. He sees himself in his front yard with a big white house behind him and a white picket fence. He is cooking on the grill, while his adopted son, wearing a

Boy Scout uniform, plays with their golden retriever in the back ground. His beautiful wife comes outside bringing him lemonade to sip on as he grills. What a beautiful picture Major Payne has painted in his own mind! However, it is not long before this beautiful imagery is infiltrated and consumed by thoughts of war. As wonderful as this day dream is, before long the fantasy has turned into a Vietnam flash back.

As foolish as this example may seem, it adequately describes the way addiction would crush my hopes and dreams of a future. I too would sit at a crossroads, envisioning the white picket fence, the wife, the kids, the happy life. However, before long my vision became blurred and distorted by the blue wax bag that dangled directly in front of my face. As much as I tried to see past it, the only reality I knew was that little blue bag containing a little brown substance. Unfortunately, the story didn't end like Major Payne's did. He chose to turn away from the war he loved, to a new life, and he pursued his dream. For me, pursuing my dream was not an option.

"I was not my own, I belonged to heroin … it was my master."

This is not to say that I didn't try and fight my way past the bag. Heaven knows that I tried. I tried quitting cold turkey on my own. I went through detox centers. I would change my people, places, and things. I left relationships that were detrimental to my sobriety. I even moved all the way out to the Midwest, to the State of Kansas, in the hope that a new location would help set me free from my enslavement to drugs. However, as an old friend once told me, "*Wherever I go, that's where I am.*"

I was basically seeking to obtain sobriety by reaching for a standard of moral goodness that I was never, ever able to obtain. The more I tried to work towards sobriety, the harder and harder I fell into addiction's unbreakable grasp. The bottom line is that none of these things worked for me. When I got out of the detox center I immediately went and purchased an 8 ball of cocaine. My many attempts at quitting cold turkey only produced a superiority complex within me that was ultimately crushed when the inevitable relapse took place. All the new girls I dated were already hooked on heroin or painkillers. If they weren't, they would be by the time we broke up. Even trying to sever ties with people, places, and things resulted in me going full circle and returning to the same situations with different faces.

A perfect example of this was my move to Kansas. I had a brilliant idea and sure concept for success in sobriety. I thought that all I had to do was move away from the place where my addiction thrived and I would be free, but I again found, "wherever I go, there I am." Three weeks after moving out to the Midwest, I met a co-worker who lived on the college campus and he invited me to come to a toga party at his house. Agreeing to come was the first step on my road back to destruction. Sure enough, I went to the party and started drinking. We became friends and partying at his house became a weekly occurrence. One week, I went up to his room with a group of people and a girl pulled out her prescription for Oxycodone. On that night, I returned to my full blown opiate addiction. I was 1,300 miles away from where my problem began, with none of my former influences around, and I was once again sniffing pain killers. Looking back now, the problem wasn't my environment or my peers. The truth is that I am the problem and the problem lives inside of me.

This reality proved itself to be true time and time again. In every circumstance and failed attempt to rid myself of this plague, the harder I worked to be good on my own, the more I failed. The more I tried to escape a life of drugs and trade it for one with a wife and children and a dog, the happy life with a white picket fence, the deeper I sunk into the pit. I eventually came to realize that I was utterly helpless and there was absolutely nothing that I could do to deliver myself from addiction.

You see, I wasn't just addicted to drugs. I was a slave of the drug. I was bound tightly by its grip and controlled by its every demand. The more I tried to escape the bondage that I was in, the harder my master would drag me back and punish me into submission. The longer this cycle went on the tighter the drugs grip was on me, until I submitted to my master's will. The drug had become my sovereign and it controlled my mind, body, and soul. I was not my own. I belonged to heroin; it was my master.

The best way to describe my circumstance is that I was a spiritual corpse and my body was the coffin.

Addiction to drugs had taken the life in my soul and I lay dead in my own coffin made of flesh. There was nothing I could do to climb out of that coffin. To make matters worse, the longer I was addicted, the more my mind and soul began to rot as a result of the lifestyle that accompanied it. As my master demanded that I satisfy its calling, I would begin to compromise my own moral compass to satisfy that urge. With each act of pursuit, my mind and soul would rot and decay until I was no longer recognizable. Eventually, I was so far gone that I began to love my master regardless of the pain and abuse it caused me. I no longer wanted to leave the tomb. I was content being spiritually dead. I was as willing and able to leave my addiction as a dead man is to walk out of his grave.

I'd often get down to my last bag of heroin and say to myself, "*This is it. I'm done. Tomorrow is going to be a new day where I have a new life.*" I would swear that this was it and I was done. In those moments, I sincerely wanted to be done with heroin and I wanted to move beyond the blue bag. Yet every time, I would wake up the next morning and go right back to the block to cop another bundle. It was almost as though the real me was trapped in the back of my subconscious and my mind was on auto pilot. In the back of my mind, it felt like I was desperately grasping onto the bars of my prison cell, screaming for help, begging and pleading with myself not to do it. But the more I screamed and the more I pleaded with myself the less it helped. My mind and body would always direct me right back to a place where I could find my next high. The more this happened, the less I would resist. This battle would continue, until all of me was gone. Eventually, I came to what I believed was the end of the road. However, this was just the beginning of what God was about to do in my life.

I can vividly remember the first time I ever examined my life and asked "How did I get here?" The setting was a detox facility outside of Wilmington, Delaware. I remember the scene as though it was yesterday. I remember the blue scrubs that I wore as I sat on the thin mattress on the bed. It was down time in the detox center, so everyone was required to go lie down and rest. The only light in the room cast shadows on the floor as it pushed through the blinds on the window. For the first time in so long, the world had gone silent and I was alone. Not alone in the sense of not having human interaction, but alone in the sense that I had nothing and no one imposing upon me. It was the first time since adolescence that my mind wasn't under the influence of any type of mind-altering drug and none of the usual influential factors were weighing on my thoughts. The only voice that I could hear was the one inside my own head. Some of you who read this know the feeling and the picture being painted all too well. It feels almost like time has stopped, and in that moment, the past 10 years of my life came crashing into my present reality with soul crushing force. It was at that point that I first asked the question, "*How did I get here?*"

The story is quite common among others who are bound in addiction. When I was in middle school, there was an anti-drug program that included a police officer who came into the school every so often to talk to the children about the dangers of using drugs. I remember the officer stating the dangers of marijuana and that it would ultimately destroy our lives. But then I smoked marijuana and realized it didn't immediately cause the total collapse of my existence. Instead, after smoking marijuana for the first time, all I did was laugh hysterically and gorge on junk food. As a preteen, smoking weed was ridiculously fun. What I failed to realize was that in my new found love for smoking weed, I had lost my fear of the potential effects of getting high.

My mindset was, *"If weed makes me feel this good, imagine how harder drugs must feel!"* The next drug I tried was psilocybin, which made me feel like I was spiritually on another plane of existence. And from there, I went on to try cocaine. Then I decided to try acid. Acid turned into PCP, and PCP turned into Ecstasy, which turned into trying meth. Meth turned into general pill usage, and pills narrowed -down to opioid pain killers, which ultimately turned into heroin.

During the time that this picture was taken, I was coming to the end of a 4 day drug binge.

2

---●---

Darker and Darker and Darker

You can't really speak about drug addiction unless you have gone through it. Family, friends, and experts all try to understand what those in addiction are experiencing. But they will never truly grasp the absolute horror that it inflicts on those who are in it. There is a unique and bizarre fear associated with drug addiction that engulfs every aspect of the addict's being. This is especially true when it comes to being hooked on opioids.

Every addict knows this fear! Think back to times when you would call your dealer and he didn't answer or needed to re-up. Perhaps the circumstance was that you had no money and the dealer wouldn't front you the drugs. The fear onsets in circumstances when the drug demanded that you use it and you didn't have the means to do so. The fear begins with the onset of an anxiety that feels as though it is pulsing through your veins to the core of your very soul.

The weight of this fear is unexplainable, especially when viewed by those outside of addiction. Often loved ones will question why the addict doesn't "*just stop using.*" Such a statement is made from a perspective of ignorance – one that can only see one aspect of suffering the addict goes through. Those outside of addiction can only understand what they see manifested through the addict's physical withdrawal symptoms. They can understand and relate to diarrhea, muscle cramps, nausea, and sleeplessness, but someone who has never been an addict can never grasp what happens inside the soul of an addict going through withdrawal.

"I was a slave to opioids.
The soul in me had submitted to it.
Heroin had become my master."

Physical withdrawal is nothing compared to the torment that takes place in the heart of an addict who can't feed their need. The desperation and anxiety experienced is excruciating. In my own personal circumstance, it felt as though I was having my one true love ripped from me and murdered before my very eyes. In that moment, I would do anything to have my love back for just one moment! I would give my money, my health, my morals, my life, and my own soul to just have my love back for even a moment.

When I finally got the drug in my system, it was as though my true love had been raised from the dead and given back to me. But in the moment when the initial rush of the drug faded, she was slowly ripped from my arms again. I watched her die all over again, and my soul within me was torn to pieces by the anguish.

This is the slavery of addiction! At the beginning of my addiction, this feeling was tolerable. I could somewhat function and fake as though I was not torn apart inside. Within a month of consistent usage the feeling was all consuming. Within six months, I had grown to fear withdrawal to the point that I was no longer using for the high but to escape the terror that awaited me. This is why people turn to prostitution, robbery, and a plethora of other devious schemes to obtain their drug of choice.

The horror of addiction is all-consuming. It devours both body and mind. It wraps its fingers around the heart of those it captures and squeezes until they have nothing left. I was a slave to opioids. The soul in me had submitted to it. Heroin had become my master.

So there I was, sitting in that dark room in the detox center at 19 years of age, and it was the first time since I was a child that I wasn't on drugs. It was here that the reality that I was a junkie hit me. And man did it hit me hard. I was scared, confused, helpless, hopeless and hollow all at the same time. As I pondered my existence and examined my past, it caused my mind to go into a tail spin as I tried to grasp how I got into this predicament.

I had grown up in a Christian family with good parents. They did their absolute best and although they had their faults, they did their best to raise me right. When I was a child they were new in their faith and quite zealous about it. They had found hope and life in Jesus. On the other hand, even as a child, I hated the concept of Jesus and especially my parents' love for

Him. Looking back, it deeply saddens me to see how dark my heart was as a child and how I poured that anger out on those who loved me the most.

Like many people who "find Jesus," my parents' zeal for Him and love for me drove them to want to see me and everyone else get saved. In other words, they were stone cold "Bible-thumpers." Every conversation with everyone was about Jesus. My dad would often try to proselytize the servers at restaurants by leaving a Bible-tract or telling them that Jesus died for them. For an 11-year old kid, there is only one word to describe such behavior – humiliating. They even pulled me out of public school and placed me into a Christian school, and I hated it. I hated the kids, I hated the teachers, and I hated having Jesus shoved down my throat every day. It was "Jesus" everywhere I turned! In my home, in my school, Jesus was literally everywhere.

I was an angry child, and angry for no reason, with no justification for why I was so miserable. It almost seemed like the more Jesus was talked about, the blacker my heart got. It may seem strange to speak of a child that has barely made it into his teens as having a black heart. But with each reference to Jesus, my resentment grew and my heart was hardened. This escalated to the point that I could no longer attend the Christian school and was returned to public school. The problem here was that I was so isolated in the Christian school from the other children that my social skills had deteriorated. Once I was back in a public school, I felt insecure and was unable to establish healthy relationships. This all changed once I found my social home. This social home was amongst the stoner kids at school.

I fit right into this social circle since all they did was smoke weed, listen to music, and watch pro wrestling. They were hardcore fans of the music group the Insane Clown Posse, which promoted sex, drugs, and violence to the extreme. It was the perfect fantasy world for me to escape into and away from the reality that surrounded me. In this social context there was no pressure to fit in, no pressure to conform, and most importantly no Jesus. It was the perfect circumstance for me at the age of 13 and cultivated the ever expanding darkness within my soul.

While this may have just seemed like harmless adolescent fun, with each step down this path, I was one step closer to destruction. The extent of my drug usage progressed rapidly and so did the depths of my depravity as I was overtaken by this lifestyle. What was once weed, music and pro wrestling were now suicidal thoughts, violent tendencies and a full-blown opioid addiction.

3

The Bible and a Detox Center

Being in the position that I am now, I have the opportunity to look on my life and see the bigger picture of what was happening. I always assumed that all the Jesus talk and Bible thumping was nothing more than foolish words that were going in one ear and out the other. The only bit of Jesus that was retained within me was just so I could hate Him and the Christian message all the more. What I failed to realize was that every time my parents, teachers, pastors, and other Christians mentioned Jesus and what He did on the cross for me, seeds were being sown on my heart. Through all these years those seeds of the gospel laid dormant, waiting for the moment when God would interject Himself into my life and cause them to take root.

So there I was, alone with my thoughts in the corner of a dark room in the detox center. I was consumed by absolute horror and harsh reality of realizing the fact that I was a fiend. And in the midst of my mental anarchy, I glanced over at the shelf in my room and all the chaos stopped. On that shelf was a Bible. I picked the Bible up and sat back down on my bed. For the first few minutes, I just sat and stared at it. I had no idea how to handle this book or how to read it, yet I couldn't help myself from curiously examining its contents. I opened to the first verse of the first chapter in the first book, Genesis 1:1, *"In the beginning, God created the heavens and the earth."* During the rest of my stay in the detox center, I isolated myself in my living quarters and spent my time reading intently.

During this time of study, my mind continued in its whirlwind of thought. However, the object of my thought was no longer my addiction or questioning how I ended up as a junkie. Instead, my mind was flooded with all the things people had told me about Jesus. All those times – the Bible thumping, all the Christian zeal, and the entire message of Jesus' death, burial, and resurrection – came charging out of my subconscious and straight into the forefront of my mind as I read through the scriptures. The more I read, the more I couldn't help but know that it was true – and I believed.

Certainly this must have been the end of the story – right? I got saved, changed my ways, was completely healed, and was on my way to that white picket fence? The simple answer is no. I didn't even complete the entire detox program. On the fifth day, I grew weary of sitting in that dark room and wanted to leave. That same day, I checked out of the detox center against medical advice and went to get an 8 ball of coke. Just a few days later, I was dropping acid and had returned to my lifestyle of promiscuous drug abuse. And so it seemed that just as quickly as Jesus came upon me, Jesus was gone, forced to the back of my subconscious and never to be spoken of again.

This is not the end of the story though, as something had happened inside my mind at the detox center. Even though I had left Jesus back in that facility, I left with a consciousness that reached far deeper into the depths of my soul than the hand of addiction ever could. I had been brought face to face with God's Law in the pages of that Bible, and it left my conscience scarred by the reality that I had violated every single aspect of it.

When I was in the detox center, I started reading Genesis in the Bible. I read straight through, all the way to Exodus, which explicitly revealed God's commandments by stating,

And God spoke all these words:

[2] "I am the LORD your God, who brought you out of Egypt, out of the land of slavery.

[3] "You shall have no other gods before[a] me.

[4] "You shall not make for yourself an image in the form of anything in heaven above or on the earth beneath or in the waters below. [5] You shall not bow down to them or worship them; for I, the LORD your God, am a jealous God, punishing the children for the sin of the parents to the third and fourth generation of those who hate me, [6] but showing love to a thousand generations of those who love me and keep my commandments.

[7] *"You shall not misuse the name of the LORD your God, for the LORD will not hold anyone guiltless who misuses his name.*

[8] *"Remember the Sabbath day by keeping it holy.* [9] *Six days you shall labor and do all your work,* [10] *but the seventh day is a sabbath to the LORD your God. On it you shall not do any work, neither you, nor your son or daughter, nor your male or female servant, nor your animals, nor any foreigner residing in your towns.* [11] *For in six days the LORD made the heavens and the earth, the sea, and all that is in them, but he rested on the seventh day. Therefore the LORD blessed the Sabbath day and made it holy.*

[12] *"Honor your father and your mother, so that you may live long in the land the LORD your God is giving you.*

[13] *"You shall not murder.*

[14] *"You shall not commit adultery.*

[15] *"You shall not steal.*

[16] *"You shall not give false testimony against your neighbor.*

[17] *"You shall not covet your neighbor's house. You shall not covet your neighbor's wife, or his male or female servant, his ox or donkey, or anything that belongs to your neighbor."*

[18] When the people saw the thunder and lightning and heard the trumpet and saw the mountain in smoke, they trembled with fear. They stayed at a distance [19] and said to Moses, "Speak to us yourself and we will listen. But do not have God speak to us or we will die."

[20] Moses said to the people, "Do not be afraid. God has come to test you, so that the fear of God will be with you to keep you from sinning."

(Exodus 20:1-20)

I had heard about these commandments years before and now an awareness of them had been burned into the depths of my soul. These words would haunt me constantly in the quiet moments when I had no way to hide from my thoughts. Every single night, I would have to self-medicate to the point that I would black out because I knew that if I was alone in my own head – His Law was there waiting for me.

You may think to yourself, "*So what?   The Bible gives us a bunch of commands.   That is nothing to fear.*" I agree, there is no reason to fear God's laws if we have kept them.   But in my addiction I had violated every single one of these laws, hundreds if not thousands of times on a daily basis since I started using drugs.   This does not include all of the violations that I committed during my adolescent years prior to drug abuse. Looking at my own personal abuse of God's Law:

- 1st and 2nd Commandments: On a daily basis for the duration of my addiction, I worshiped drugs as a god in my life.

- 3rd Commandment: By worshipping something other than God as a god on a daily basis, I was blaspheming God by stating that something other than him is worthy of my praise.

- 4th Commandment: I never rested from my pursuit of drugs, not even when I lay down to sleep at night. From the moment I awoke, I worked to get high. At the moment I laid down, I was thinking about the next day's work.

- 5th Commandment: I constantly dishonored my mother and father through lying, stealing, and abusiveness towards them as I chased the drug. In my addiction, I viewed my family as objects to be manipulated as a means to satisfy my slave master's demand. This even included threatening to commit suicide if they didn't give me money.

- 6th Commandment: Though I never actually committed physical murder, the Bible teaches that sin begins in the heart and in the mind, and even if you hate someone it is as though you are a murderer in your heart (1 John 3:15; Matthew 5:21-23).

31

Just imagine, a fellow addict hits you up and says they can get bundles for $25. You've been hustling all day to get enough to get high and you know this is too good to be true. Yet if this is true, you can get double the amount of dope for the same price. However, this fellow addict states, *"The dealer is real shady and doesn't want anyone knowing who he is, so you have to give me the money up front."* You know that you are about to get played, but you take the risk due to the deal being too good to pass up. Imagine you give the money to the fellow addict and he doesn't show up in the time frame that he said he would. You call him and he states that the dealer, *"hasn't hit me back yet."* Another half hour and you call again. No answer. Another half hour and you call again, only to find the fellow addict has turned off his phone. Think about that moment and the fact that you got burned. Tell me the hatred in your heart wasn't so intense that you would have killed the other addict in that moment if you could have.

- 7th Commandment: This will be discussed in greater detail later, but in my addiction I found that the deeper I went into addiction, the more my sexual morale decayed and the darker and more depraved my sex life became.

- 8th Commandment: Does stealing to enable an addiction need any further explanation? Let's move on.

- 9th Commandment: In my addiction, lying became more common than speaking the truth. Whether it was a lie to manipulate money out of people, keep up a positive appearance, or cover past lies, lying became my default mode of speech and I became a master of the craft.

- 10th Commandment: I can't tell you how often I coveted others in my addiction. I would be jealous of those who had prescriptions to pain killers. I have a friend who broke his leg at a concert and received a prescription. I cannot tell you how this changed our friendship and how I would have given both legs and my back for that script.

Now looking back on my 12 years of drug abuse, let's assume that I broke every one of these commandments a minimum of once a day, every day for those 12 years. That is 10 violations a day at 365 days a year, for 14 years – that is 43,800 violations of God's Law!

Allow me to paint a picture for you. Imagine that you are having a bad day and a mall security guard says something that causes you to snap and you slap them in the face. What is going to happen? You will be arrested, charged, and go to jail. Now imagine that the police show up and attempt to arrest you, so you resist arrest and begin slapping them in the face as well. What is going to happen? You would most likely be shot with mace, tasered, beaten up, arrested, given more serious charges, and then placed in jail for a much longer sentence. Now imagine that you are in your cell and the President of the United States shows up at your cell door and wants to speak with you. Imagine that during this conversation the POTUS offends you and you begin slapping him silly. What's going to happen then? The Secret Service is probably going to shoot you dead!

"I had been brought face to face with God's Law in the pages of that Bible"

My point in painting this picture is to show that the more authority an individual has, the more intense the punishment is for those who offend that person. So let me ask you this. What do you think would happen if you slapped a holy and righteous God in the face? What would happen if you slapped Him 43,800 times? This was the reality that I left the detox center with. In my addiction, I had slapped God in the face over and over again and this would always be accompanied by the thought that someday I was going to die and stand before Him. He would know all of my sin and I would be held accountable for all of them.

After reading the Bible in that detox center, the thought of my sins began haunting me at night over the course of the next few years. To try and escape the reality of my sin, I'd often heavily medicate myself to the point of nodding out. Lying in bed at night, consciousness of what I had done wrong and all of the sins I was committing, tormented me, as I knew that my time was limited and that lifestyle wouldn't last forever.

How much longer could I continue getting high and pushing the boundaries of my body's limits until the day would come where I'd get high and it would be my last time?

I knew I was going to die, one way or another. On that day, I would stand before God and be held accountable for all of the horrible things I'd done in my addiction. All the lies, the crimes, the sex and the violence would demand punishment. It would all be uncovered and I would stand before Him naked in my sin. Rather than turning from my sins, however, I ran deeper and deeper into the pit of addiction and self-medication to hide from this reality.

Fast forward a few years later, and I was completely consumed by the darkness of addiction. I remember it like it was yesterday. I was lying on the floor of a trailer in Chesapeake City, Maryland. It was still dark outside. The time was approximately 5 a.m. and I was wide awake. I had no heroin and the fear of withdrawal had set in. I had no idea where I was going to get my next fix.

To make matters worse, the spiritual conviction that I'd been running from began to haunt me. My consciousness of sin and impending judgment began to overpower my fear of going through withdrawal. That was when the ever-so-small voice inside of me began telling me that it was time to get off the drugs.

I spent the next few hours fighting this voice as I lay on the floor of that trailer, trying to balance the thoughts of where I was going to get my next high with the overwhelming conviction of my sin and the command to stop using drugs. The longer this continued, the more I couldn't bear it. The next day I woke up and I made an appointment to get some medical help by using a drug called Suboxone.

4

Divine Intervention

Suboxone is a drug commonly prescribed by doctors to treat opioid addiction. It can help addicts stop using heroin, at least temporarily. Most addicts are very familiar with Suboxone, its perceived benefits, and the extreme danger associated with using it. In my case, once I got on Suboxone, I completely stopped using heroin. But one major problem that I still had was I was in a co-dependent relationship with somebody who was also addicted to heroin.

It was one of those relationships where we carried each other through our addiction. This was the type of relationship that builds its foundation on sex and drugs. It's the kind where I maintain our addiction through my job, until I get fired. Then she got a job and maintained our addiction until she got fired. And then, what happens when both partners have been fired and can't get a job? We started to scheme and plot. Just about every long-time addict can relate to this partner-in-crime relationship. It was no longer just drug addiction I was experiencing, but codependency upon this person as well. Now, all of a sudden, I had decided that I was going to use Suboxone for the rest of my life in order to stay off heroin. I had the crazy idea that I could somehow force her to get clean with me.

"Using drugs since I was 12 years old"

I had a whole game plan for how she and I were going to get clean. We would move in with my parents, get sober together, and then get jobs. Once that happened, we could move out, get married, live happily ever after, and safely exist under the safe and secure umbrella of Suboxone. In my mind, it was a picture perfect plan. What could go wrong?

It never dawned on me that I was the only one who wanted to get clean. Every addict who has been in this predicament knows what I mean. It begs the question of how I was going to try to force somebody else to get sober when I couldn't even force myself to get clean. I was too blind in my co-dependency to see that my master plan was doomed from the beginning. The more I tried pushing her to get clean the more she chased after drugs. The more I pushed the more she ran. The more she ran, the more I chased after her.

Eventually, it came to the point where I became obsessive about her. I would check text messages, emails, and Facebook. I believed that she was still using drugs after promising me she wasn't, and it became my obsession to try and prove that she was still using them. I became so self-absorbed by the desire to catch her using drugs and forcing her to get sober that I had failed to realize that where I'd once worshipped the drugs, my worship had shifted to her. All of my efforts and attention were now directed towards catching that poor girl lying about getting high rather than trying to help her or myself.

This all culminated on a bright and sunny April day. I had attempted to enact my self-righteous plan of recovery and redemption by moving us both into my parent's house. Considering who my parents are, as good Christian people, they would not let us sleep in the same room because we weren't married. So one day I woke up in my room and went to take my Suboxone and realized 20 of my strips were missing. On the street, an entire strip will go for $10, so 20 strips were worth $200. That was more than enough to buy a few bundles of dope.

I exploded in anger as I knew that all my suspicions were right. She was getting high and I was going to prove it! At that point, I was furious. I went into the room she was staying in and tore it apart, looking for the Suboxone, heroin or any other evidence that might satisfy my own ego's desire to be right. I found no drugs, no Suboxone, and no paraphernalia. I found absolutely nothing.

In the midst of anger and anxiety over this girl, the thought began to creep into my mind and I began to think that maybe I was going crazy. My thought was that I had been getting high since I was about 12 years old and perhaps all the years of usage had done considerable damage to my brain. Perhaps I had psychological issues that were only now appearing because I was no longer self-medicating (even though I still was by using Suboxone). This struck a deep fear in me. What if I was losing my mind? What if the psychological damage was so great that it was irreversible? I began to panic as anxiety overtook me and I got in my car and began to drive. I didn't know where I was driving to – I just started driving.

As I drove, I sobbed in anguish at what I had become. I was a weak and broken boy in a man's body who was helpless, hopeless, and scared beyond belief. In that moment, I had nowhere else to turn but to the One that I had run from for so many years and had hated with a passion. For the first time in so long I began to cry out to God, franticly pleading with Him to show me that I wasn't crazy. Over and over, I begged Him to show me that I hadn't lost my mind and that I was still in there somewhere. I begged Him to show me that He was real.

In the midst of praying, in the midst of my suffering and sorrow, His Law arose in my mind. At that moment, I believed in the depths of my soul that His Law and judgment were real. However, while these truths pursued me for years, another truth arose within my soul that I had buried for so long. That truth was the cross of Jesus Christ. As that realization came to my mind, I prayed that God would show me that He was real and that I wasn't crazy so that I might turn away from the drugs, the relationship, the lifestyle, the lies, the sins – all of it – and walk with Him.

This was a good lesson for me to learn to be careful about what I prayed for. As I continued driving, about

20 minutes later, I received a text from a heroin dealer and user that we used to buy heroin from. He was on his way to a rehab center and said he was trying to make things right. He let me know that a couple weeks earlier, while I was out of town, my girlfriend had gone to him and was unable to buy any heroin, so she had sex with him in exchange for a bundle of dope.

At that moment a surreal feeling came over me that left me feeling shocked. I no longer questioned whether or not I was crazy. Nor was I angry, or even hurt for that matter. I was shocked because I was still very conscience of the prayer I had just prayed to God, *"Show me I'm not crazy. Show me you are real and I will turn from my sin and walk away from it."*

At this realization, something within me led me to drive back to my parent's house and walk upstairs into the room she was staying in again. As I stood in the doorway, looking at the chaos that I had caused, I noticed a backpack that I hadn't seen when I was in her room earlier. Inside that backpack was a makeup bag, and inside the makeup bag were two bundles of heroin and syringes.

In that moment, I normally would have exploded in a rage of self-righteous justification at the fact that I was right all along. Instead, a peace came over me that I cannot explain. I no longer cared about feeling vindicated about what my girlfriend was really doing, and I no longer cared about catching her being deceitful. In that moment, I realized the God that I believed in was real. He had just showed me He was real and something inside me changed. I met with the girl later that day, handed the heroin and syringes over to her, and said goodbye.

On that day, I turned from my own sins and purposed to walk away from drugs and the lifestyle associated with them forever. I truly believe this is the moment when I went from being spiritually dead and became spiritually alive. It was almost as if my soul was resurrected from the dead, and I believed everything that I had ever heard preached from the Bible. In that moment the spiritual light came on for me, and I was changed. I was now spiritually alive in Jesus Christ!

5

Could God Really Deliver Me?

For the next few months after being saved, life felt great. After walking away from that sinful relationship, things really began to look up for me. I got a good job that paid good money doing concrete work, which I loved to do. I also met a nice girl at a church that I had begun attending. She didn't use drugs, and she would never cheat on me to get high, or steal drugs from me. Life was good and I was happy.

However, there was still one problem. That problem was Suboxone. I still relied on this substance as a safety net to keep me free from heroin. All my faith and trust was in this drug to keep me from the deadly grip of opioids. As long as I had it I was safe. This mindset caused me to pose a question to myself, "*Did I really believe God could deliver me from years of hardcore drug addiction?*" It was easy to walk away from a girl, as co-dependency was never the big issue, at least not in comparison to walking away from over a decade of drug abuse. Out of this rationale another question arose, "*Did I really want God to deliver me?*" That was the real question, and the answer was an emphatic, "*NO!*" The truth was that I had become addicted to the Suboxone, and it had become my new heroin.

So there I was, about five or six months after starting to use Suboxone, and life was spectacular. I had a great job, lots of money, and a nice new girlfriend. Yet, in the midst of all the good, I began feeling that same conviction that I had felt earlier about heroin. I could feel that ever-so-small voice within my conscience begin to say, *"It's time to get off the drugs."*

I wrestled with God over that conviction for weeks by trying to justify my rationale for staying on Suboxone. I justified my usage by on the basis that my doctor said I would be on it for the rest of my life. Furthermore, everything from a scientific and medical perspective asserted that I'd be using Suboxone for the rest of my life. I was trying to brainwash myself into believing that if I stopped using Suboxone then a relapse was inevitable. My parents were also doing their research on Suboxone and came to the same conclusions. Their rationale was, *"Doug, let's just not take the risk. You are going to just have to be on Suboxone for the rest of your life."*

This led me to laying down the law with God and telling Him that I had made my decision to stay on Suboxone, regardless of my conviction. I had convinced myself that this was for the purpose of maintaining sobriety. But the truth was I made that decision because I liked the way it made me feel and I was getting high off it. I was in denial that I was addicted to Suboxone.

That denial continued until one day when I forgot to take my Suboxone before going to work. It just so happened that I was going to be running buckets of concrete up and down ladders all day long. My crew started working at 7 a.m., but by 9 a.m. my body was no longer able to function.

What is interesting is that the physical withdrawal hadn't even kicked in yet. In my mind, I had stressed so badly about missing my regular dose of Suboxone that I began making myself believe I was already going through withdrawal symptoms even though I wasn't. That was the moment when I realized just how tight a mental stranglehold the drug had on me. I had merely traded my worship of heroin for the worship of Suboxone and it had become my master.

I thought that I had overcome the monster that had controlled me for so long, but somehow, I had been under its control all along. In the midst of the fear and suffering, I knew that what God was saying was true. I could no longer wrestle with Him; I could no longer fight against His conviction. It was time to truly walk away from drugs.

How could I do this though? I had tried everything and even my most successful attempt had secretly placed me in servitude to my addiction. I knew that getting off Suboxone was going to be horrific and excruciating. Furthermore, I knew that there was no way I could continue working while trying to get off the drug. In addition, I knew the girl I was dating at church would never understand the monster that was about to be ripped out of me. I knew I was helpless to save myself and the good life I was experiencing while taking the Suboxone. So I began to pray that the Lord would make a way for me to come off of the drugs and remove anything that stood in the way. God answered this prayer shortly afterward. I was laid off from my job and dumped by my girlfriend on the same day. In summary, the Lord had paved the way.

Previously such events would have been a trigger for me to relapse and question what the point of trying to quit drugs was. However, God had begun working in me. He was changing my heart. I didn't see these events as an opportunity to justify any drug relapse. Instead, I saw these circumstances as an answer to my prayers.

Everybody was telling me that if I tried getting off Suboxone I was going to fall back into drug addiction. I too understood this from the literature I'd read. But I also knew that my God went before me. I knew that my God that was bigger than my addiction. I had seen Him work in my life and I believed that everything He said about Himself in the Bible was true. I went home that day and I took my Suboxone into the backyard, with my parents pleading with me to keep just one strip, just in case. That day, I poured gasoline on my Suboxone prescription and I lit it on fire.

It was like the story of David and Goliath in the Bible (1 Samuel 17). There I was – weak, broken, and scared – with this colossal monster standing before me. Everyone told me that I would not be able to conquer the giant, and that if I tried to go toe to toe with my addiction, I would be crushed by its force and fall right back into a relapse.

They were absolutely right! I was no match for my addiction and I was going to be destroyed. However, in this analogy, I was not David. I was one of the scared and weak Israelites, standing far off, watching the battle. Jesus is the David character in this story, and He went before me to cut off and crush the head of the addiction Goliath that tormented me!

"What was different this time?"

What was different this time, apart from those times in the past when I'd try to quit drugs cold turkey, was that the ultimate determining factor was not me. The determining factor was Christ's crucifixion. For years, I had tried to get sober on my own. For years, I tried to detox by relying on my own strength. But this time, I knew what Jesus had done for me.

I wasn't delivered by coming to Jesus. I was delivered when Jesus came to me! He came in the midst of my pain, my suffering, and my despair. In the late nights of crying out to God during the moments when the physical and mental withdrawal was more than I could bear, He sustained me. When I felt hopeless, I found hope in Jesus. He came to me at a time when I could not do anything for myself. Jesus came to me regardless of my sins and regardless of my failures. In spite of me, He came to me. And the grace that He gave to me through His work on the cross, this is what I truly believe was the missing component in all my previous attempts to get off drugs that failed. All of my previous efforts were null and void because the critical component of deliverance from my addiction was missing. And that critical component was Jesus.

So here I am now, many years past those long sleepless nights and far beyond the grasp of addiction's enslaving hand upon me. Victory was won by Jesus and by His death, burial, and resurrection; He has removed the shackles that addiction had bound me with.

Today, the Lord has placed me in a position where I can share the same truth about addiction that has freed me from its grasp with those still in bondage to it. I will do so by using the Bible to reveal the power of God to save men from not only bondage to drugs, but all things that enslave men.

My intent in writing this book is to go beyond the surface of drug addiction and to reveal the heart of what leads to addiction. Let's talk about the bondage of addiction and discover the power of God in breaking its shackles, using the Bible in the hope that those who read this book will come to the realization that it is by nothing but Jesus and His work on the cross by which you can be truly free from the bondage of your drug of choice.

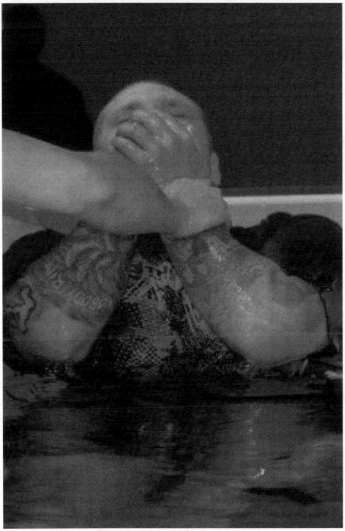

My baptism, shortly after my deliverance from my addiction to Suboxone.

6

The Bible Doesn't Talk
About Addiction... Does It?

There is a common cliché found amongst those in recovery. Almost every addict who achieves two to three weeks of sobriety has thought, *"I'm going to become a drug and alcohol counselor and save the world!"* If you have ever thought this, don't feel bad. So did I. I was no different. You see, God was moving in my life, and, just like many other addicts, I felt drawn to the idea of working with those struggling with their addiction.

I was determined in my heart to find the cure to this *"disease,"* so that I could save the world from its oppression! Rather than the usual outcome that follows these thoughts (relapse), I enrolled myself in college.

This was eight years after I had dropped out of high school. It was an absolutely horrifying idea, but I felt called to help those who had struggled in the same situation that I had experienced. I enrolled in a Bachelor of Science in Psychology program with a major in substance abuse recovery.

My goal was to help every single addict that I could, and I had aspirations that someday maybe I would help solve the addiction crisis that our country is facing. So I dove head first into my studies of addiction. It was here that my eyes were opened to the truth about "recovery."

"The truth regarding addiction and human beings"

During my studies, I came to find that there was much I had to learn about addiction before I could ever help anybody. So I began by engulfing myself in education and actively chasing this goal. The majority of the courses that I took that first year were in psychology. As I dove deeper into this topic, I realized that science and psychology couldn't adequately answer all the questions that I had regarding addiction.

Psychology could answer why our brains react in certain ways in response to certain chemicals, and it could explain why our bodies physically go through withdrawal when we don't have a substance in our system. But psychology couldn't answer why a person would sell their body sexually in pursuit of a drug. It couldn't explain why addiction turns the human mind into a prison cell. Psychology doesn't give insight into why addiction causes people to do what they don't want to do and why they do what they do when they often don't want to do it.

Psychology doesn't answer how a drug breaks a person into submission and complacency in their suffering. It can't adequately explain why a person would sell everything they have in pursuit of a drug, or why they would permanently sacrifice their health by sharing dirty needles. It doesn't tell us why an addict is often willing to give up their children, their house, their job, their sexuality, and their morality in order to get high. It doesn't tell us why a person would give up their very soul in pursuit of drugs.

As I began studying substance abuse treatment and recovery, what I came to find in my college textbooks is that the study of addiction is flawed and inconclusive. It hasn't been figured out and solved, nor is there an answer to the fact that addiction is actually an enigma to the secular world.

Here are a couple quotes from one of my textbooks:

> *"If you were to devote or if you were a devotee of television talk shows or read a small sample of the self-help books that line the bookstore shelves, you would easily be left with the impression that research has discovered the causes of, and the treatment for, alcoholism and addiction to the other drugs of abuse. Unfortunately, nothing could be further from the truth. Much of what is known about SUDs, or substance use disorders, is based on mistaken assumptions, distorted data, clinical myths and theories, or, in many cases, incomplete data."* (p.16, Concepts of Chemical

Dependency 8th Edition, Harold E. Doweiko)

"Thus, much of what we think we know about substance use disorders is not based on scientific research but on assumptions, guesses, and limited data. However, it is on this foundation that an entire rehabilitation industry has been based. It is not the purpose of this text is to deny that SUDs cause a terrible cost in individual suffering into society. That, hopefully, the reader has heard to understand how little is really known about SUDs." (Ibid, p. 17)

I remember still being a new student in college and new to the world of actual drug treatment and reading this – and just being astounded. My assumption coming into the study of addiction is that there are scientific principles at work in Alcoholics Anonymous and Narcotics Anonymous and other treatment programs. I had assumed these various programs offered to addicts meant that science and psychology had solved the addiction problem, or at least had a grasp of it. As I continued to study and read about addiction in my textbooks, I realized there was so much that was unknown about the topic and that most of what is accepted in recovery is based on assumptions and not facts.

On the other hand, psychology was not the only topic that I began studying during that first year. I was simultaneously taking courses in theology. What I found was that as I studied theology, along with science and psychology, all the questions psychology couldn't answer about addiction, the Bible could. Furthermore, as I examined theology, I began to realize what it was in me that kept me in bondage to addiction for all those years.

The deeper I went the clearer the picture became. And it went beyond my addiction. This went to my human condition in general and the consequences of it. This had such a profound effect upon my life and my understanding of the human existence that I transferred my degree program from psychology to theology. The primary reason for this was a pursuit of the truth regarding addiction and human beings' relationships with God.

"Does the Bible actually talk about addiction?"

This brings us to the question, *"Where does the Bible actually talk about addiction?"* Does it directly mention drug addiction? This is a question I am asked regularly by the people I interact with, and the simple answer is, *"Yes."* However, uncovering this answer takes a little bit of effort.

Before we address where addiction is talked about in the Bible, we have to take into account the gap between us and the authors. The Bible was written nearly 2,000 years ago, in a completely different culture, with different morals, standards, and norms compared to ours. It was also written for people facing a particular set of circumstances, and written in a language that is drastically different than ours.

In order to see where addiction is found in scripture, we have to go beneath its surface and step into the shoes of the original writers and their audience. We have to try and understand biblical passages in the way that they would have been originally understood before we try to apply their meaning to ourselves.

So where in the Bible is addiction spoken of? Addiction is spoken of specifically in Galatians 5: 19-21. The writer of this passage is the apostle Paul and he is speaking to a group of Christians. Paul is explaining that there is a war that takes place within Christians between the Holy Spirit and their sinful human nature, with its evil desires. By their expression of these two realities, Christians can gauge the authenticity of their salvation or see if they are dominated by sinful human nature.

Verses 19-21 give a list of sins that show evidence of the work of "the flesh," which reveal sinful human nature. So where in this verse does it mention drug use? In order to see drug use, we have to go back to the original language in which the New Testament was written, Koine Greek.

Galatians 5: 19-21 (English Standard Version) says, *"Now the works of the flesh are evident: sexual immorality, impurity, sensuality, idolatry, sorcery, enmity, strife, jealousy, fits of anger, rivalries, dissensions, divisions, envy, drunkenness, orgies, and things like these. I warn you, as I warned you before, that those who do such things will not inherit the kingdom of God."*

So where does this verse speak about addiction? Verse 20 mentions the word "sorcery." In some translations, the word is translated as "witchcraft." When most of us think of witchcraft we think of magic spells, black cats and cauldrons filled with potions. We think of the Wizard of Oz and movies like Hocus Pocus. But when we take this word sorcery or witchcraft in English and look back at that the Greek root, it's translated from the word "pharmakeia."

Pharmakeia is actually where we actually get our English word "pharmacy" from. This term originally referred to the administration of medication in general. However, as time went on, and the word evolved, it grew to reference poisonous and mind-altering substances specifically used in religious and ritualistic ceremonies. In other words, it refers to drugs that altered the mind and mood of those taking them. This word is used three times in the New Testament (Gal. 5:20; Rev. 9:21; 18:23), and each time, it's used in reference to an act that brings about God's judgment against the wicked.

One big question many Christians then have is whether or not a person can be truly saved if they ever use pharmakeia. I think it's important to distinguish between having used a drug and drug addiction. These are two distinct and very different things.

So how is this passage to be understood? Is a professing Christian not really saved if they ever smoke a joint? Or what about a Christian who has cancer and takes OxyContin for pain? Does Galatians 5: 19-21 teach that if a Christian ever takes a drug then it's a sign they're not really saved? The simple answer is "No." But again, we must go beneath the surface to see how the original language expresses this.

If we go down the passage to where it says, "those who do such things will not inherit the kingdom of God," the phrase "do such things" is derived from the Greek word "prassontes." In some translations the English equivalent means "practice" or "live like this." In other words the Greek word behind this phrase paints the picture of something that is being done habitually and continually in the present tense. So when we apply it to pharmakeia, drug use, it paints a picture of someone who is continually poisoning themselves with a mind-altering substance over and over and over again on a daily basis. It is not a one-time instance, or even a past instance, that Paul has in mind. Rather, he is looking at pharmakeia that is done continually in the present tense. The first time I saw this, my mind was blown because this is what addiction is all about! This takes me back to the words of a friend of mine, who is now deceased. He stated to me, "*There is no recreational or medical usage of OxyContin. OxyContin is a lifestyle.*" According to the Bible, those who live such a lifestyle "*will not inherit the kingdom of God.*"

7

So What's the Big Deal?

At this point you may be asking yourself, "Why is addiction morally wrong?" In essence, you're asserting that it's a person's choice whether they want to use drugs over and over and over again. Furthermore, what gives the apostle Paul, or anyone for that matter, the right to dictate what I put into my body? This is an excellent and critical question to understanding the depths of our addiction. Why is addiction wrong? The first step in understanding this question is to realize that the issue of addiction goes deeper than an individual's habitual drug use.

Addiction is a lifestyle. It consumes everything in one's life. Go to the heroin addict who is homeless on Kensington Avenue in Philadelphia or living in a tent in Los Angeles and ask them how they got there. Ask them what they have lost in pursuit of their addiction. Every situation is different, of course, but many stories are very much the same. In pursuit of the drugs, the addict gives up their health, family, friends, jobs, homes, identity, dreams, morals and all hope that they have had.

SO WHAT'S THE BIG DEAL?

Think of a mother with beautiful children who, in the midst of her addiction, has lost all desire to raise them. Think of a person on a path towards achieving their career goals who, in the midst of addiction, gives up all of their dreams. Each story differs, but they are also strangely the same. Addiction does not discriminate and it unifies its victims by the path of destruction that it tears through their lives. Yet for some reason, the mom won't stop using and the go-getter will only go get high. Why is this?

What we have to realize is that addiction goes beyond mere drug use. It becomes a form of worship. Addiction isn't the problem in and of itself. Addiction is merely the symptom of a much larger predicament. It's an external expression of a much deeper and darker issue lurking in the hearts of men.

When we as Christians look at addiction we may ask if merely giving up drugs is enough to satisfy a person. Is getting high the end goal, or is maintaining sobriety merely treating the symptoms without curing the cancer? There are certainly people who have stopped using drugs after going through treatment programs, or working the 12-step programs, or establishing attachments to new people or new places. Such things may be beneficial in treating the symptoms of addiction, but true freedom requires going much deeper beyond the surface.

"The core issue of addiction is not drug use -- it is idolatry!"

You see, the heart of addiction can be seen in Exodus 20: 3-6 (ESV). *"You shall have no other gods before me. You shall not make for yourself a carved image, or any likeness of anything that is in heaven above, or that is in the earth beneath, or that is in the water under the earth. You shall not bow down to them or serve them, for I the LORD your God am a jealous God, visiting the iniquity of the fathers on the children to the third and the fourth generation of those who hate me, but showing steadfast love to thousands of those who love me and keep my commandments."*

Exodus 20:3-6 refers to the first two of God's Ten Commandments. And God's command of first importance is that man will have no other gods before Him. And God also commands that mankind will not take anything in this world and make it into an image that they worship.

In the simplest terms what this means is that we are not to take anything in this life and make it an object of worship. But isn't this is exactly what we do when we are in our addictions? We take a substance, which is an inanimate object, and we offer everything that is precious to us to it in worshipful sacrifice.

In our worship of the drug we offer our relationships with our children by neglecting them, even to the point of fully losing them as we chase a drug. We offer our health through sharing needles, or our bodies through prostitution. We offer our money and assets to continually have this little, cheap god in our possession. We offer the relationships with our families by lying, cheating, and stealing from them in order to come back to our little, cheap god's altar. We offer our soul by laying aside our morals to go deeper in worship to the god of our addiction. And we offer our lives giving everything we have physically, mentally, and spiritually on the altar of the drug of our choice. The core issue of addiction is not drug use – it is idolatry!

So then we have to ask what the drug itself is. Does heroin eat? Does it sleep? Does it breathe? Does it love you? Does it care about you? Does heroin hate you? Does a drug feel any emotion when you leave your children in order to pursue it? Does heroin comfort someone after they sell their body for the next fix? Does any drug cry with the person addicted to it when the test results show they've contracted HIV because they shared a needle with an infected user? Does any drug seek an addict out to give itself to the one who is tormented in the midst of withdrawal? The answer to all of these questions is, "No." A person's drug of choice is an inanimate object and has no life of its own.

The same pain killer that an addict worships for evil serves a purpose of good when it helps ease the pain of a person dying from cancer. Drugs have no life in themselves, but somehow, they have the power to consume an addict's life. So an addict has to ask what the power is behind the drug that they are worshipping.

If we look at 1 Corinthians 10: 19-22 (ESV), it says, *"What do I imply then? That food offered to idols is anything, or that an idol is anything? No, I imply that what pagans sacrifice they offer to demons and not to God. I do not want you to be participants with demons. You cannot drink the cup of the Lord and the cup of demons. You cannot partake of the table of the Lord and the table of demons. Shall we provoke the Lord to jealousy? Are we stronger than he?"*

What Paul is saying in this passage of scripture is that he knows idols are nothing. Physically, they are neither moral nor immoral in themselves, just like any drug is not moral or immoral in and of itself. Drugs are neutral and inanimate objects. The problem arises when a person begins to worship, sacrifices and makes an offering to the idol of their respective drug. In doing this they are actually offering themselves to demonic forces that stand behind that drug.

This can be seen in Deuteronomy 32: 16-17 (ESV), where the Israelites provoke God to anger by chasing after strange gods and sacrificing to the demons behind them. *"They stirred him to jealousy with strange gods; with abominations they provoked him to anger. They sacrificed to demons that were no gods, to gods they had never known, to new gods that had come recently, whom your fathers had never dreaded."*

Addiction might be illustrated in the following way. Think of a gazelle in Africa. Imagine the sun is hot and it's beating down on the gazelle. The gazelle becomes thirsty and its mouth is parched. All the gazelle wants is a drink of refreshing water. This water is neither good nor bad in itself. The gazelle comes to the edge of the watering hole and bows its head down. It kneels down and puts its lips in the cool water. It begins to drink and, oh, how satisfying the water is as it hits the gazelle's lips. It moisturizes its tongue and the gazelle drinks and drinks and drinks. How satisfying it is – until the gazelle lifts its eyes up and sees the crocodile that is lying in the water before it. As the gazelle looks into the cold eyes of the crocodile, and before it can pull away, it is too late. The croc grabs the gazelle and drags it into the water, drowning it prior to eating.

Oh how wonderful heroin felt the first time I used it. I felt as though all my problems had been solved. The thirst in my soul was seemingly quenched and I was in ecstasy. With each drink the pain of this world seemed to drift away. So I continued to drink more and more, until the moment I lifted my head from the water and I was dragged by the monster living within into the depths. Such is the case when we offer ourselves on the altar of demons. We are trapped. We are grabbed by the demon and dragged into the depths of our addiction. Addicts become prisoners of their own minds. No matter how much pain and suffering they endure, they fall more and more in love with their idol. And they are never satisfied.

8

Why do we Chase After Idols?

The summer of 2017 was a rough season for Rock n' Roll. During that summer, it lost two of its most prestigious artists within 30 years: Chris Cornell and Chester Bennington.

Chris Cornell had multiple studio albums and had won multiple music awards. His net worth was listed at 60 million dollars. Chris Cornell seemingly had everything a man could want. He had sex, drugs, and rock and roll at his disposal. But along with his studio albums and his awards and his millions of dollars, Chris also carried with him suffering that was caused by depression and addiction. On May 17th, 2017, Chris Cornell committed suicide by hanging himself.

Chester Bennington, of the band, Linkin Park, had also released multiple studio albums. He had won over 50 music awards and his net worth was listed at 27 million dollars. Just like Chris Cornell, amidst all of his worldly success, he also suffered from depression and addiction. On July 20th 2017, he too committed suicide by hanging.

These two suicides caused me to research other celebrity suicides in the past few years. The most astounding was that of Robin Williams. Robin Williams appeared in over 100 productions in TV, movies, standup comedy specials, and even one video game. He had 14 different entertainment awards and a net worth of over $100 million dollars. And it appears that yearly, he helped raise $80 million for charities. And yet, amidst all of his success, all that he had done, the way people praised him and loved him, Robin Williams struggled with depression and addiction. In 2014, he too committed suicide by hanging.

These are just a few examples of men who accomplished amazing things. Looking at their lives, it would appear that they had the potential to have anything that their hearts could have desired. Yet, they were so dissatisfied that they saw death as a better option that continuing to live. This presents us with a very harsh truth for our own lives. If these men could not find satisfaction in all that this world has to offer, then perhaps we may ask ourselves, "Why?"

"A drug that is worshipped"

As wealthy as these individuals were, however, they still didn't compare, to the biblical character named Solomon. Solomon was Israel's most prosperous king. He was rich beyond your, mine, and Robin Williams' wildest dreams combined. He also had 300 wives and 700 concubines. Most men struggle with having one woman, but Solomon had more women than any man could dream of handling. He was the only king of Israel who experienced complete peace during his reign and he had no worries. By God's hand Solomon also became the wisest man alive.

Solomon had anything that his heart desired. Yet when we look at Ecclesiastes 1, written by Solomon, what do we read? We see great sorrow. Solomon's worldview saw life as being one of vanity, like a breath that comes and then vanishes without meaning. He described life as generations coming and going, day after day, simply passing by without purpose. He saw life as fleeting, simply passing by. Eventually death comes, and those who were once alive are simply forgotten. He felt as if everything that one strives for in this life is meaningless. Time passes, and all of one's future plans become lost in the past. He simply concludes there is nothing new under the sun. What is new eventually becomes old. And as soon as one's hopes and dreams become a reality they immediately become the past and fly away. In this dim view of life, once the future becomes the past it becomes worthless. And once it's worthless, one simply seeks the next thing to try and quench their soul's thirst.

As human beings we strive for goal after goal, seeking to satisfy the desires of our souls. However, after we reach those goals, after we reach the top of the mountain, what we find is that the view is not as enticing as the next mountain we see. And then we want to climb to the top of that one. We hunger and desire for more and more, but we are never satisfied.

I personally experienced this in the pursuit of my undergraduate degree in theology. In chasing this goal I strived, and I fought, and I scratched, and I clawed to the end. I spent late nights working a full-time job while enrolled in full-time schooling so that I could get on to the football field, in my cap and gown, by a certain date. I got to walk the graduation stage and stood among theologians and received my diploma. I even got to shake the hands of many of those theologians. On that day, I conquered the mountain before me and reached the top of my goals! And then I woke up the next day and it was over. No more football field, no more handshakes, and my diploma was just a piece of paper. The only thing that I could think about now was the next goal to accomplish. What would be the next mountain that I would climb?

Solomon's passage in Ecclesiastes describes what I felt after chasing my college degree. It is similar to the affliction of an addict. This same feeling isn't limited to just drug abusers. It can be seen in every area of the human life. All men and women are plagued by vain pursuits that leave them feeling hollow.

For drug addicts, one is too many and a thousand is never enough. Day after day is spent scratching and clawing to grasp hold of a drug that is worshipped. After the momentary fix is attained the addict immediately thinks about how to get the next fix.

The sex addict pursues a moment of pleasure, but upon climax the satisfaction becomes a memory. And thus, they move on in search of another temporary fix with another person.

The person who is addicted to their work daily breaks their back. They spend their time, day after day, week after week, striving for the next pay day. By the time they receive the paycheck that they have slaved for, their bills have consumed every penny and there is absolutely nothing left over to enjoy.

Others obsessively seek companionship. They search in pursuit of a person that they believe will fill the void in their heart. Once they find the person they think will fulfill their soul, they discover that individual cannot satisfy it. Short is the honeymoon period where everything is great, and they are happy, and they feel constant love for this person. Reality checks in and eventually the excitement of the new relationship dies and they are left to pursue another relationship.

Solomon describes vain pursuit in Ecclesiastes 1:7-8 (ESV). He wrote, "*All streams run to the sea, but the sea is not full; to the place where the streams flow, there they flow again. All things are full of weariness; a man cannot utter it; the eye is not satisfied with seeing, nor the ear filled with hearing.*" In other words, human beings are like the ocean. We humans constantly take in our fill, but we are never full. Just like the human eye, which takes in the beauty of the world it views, it is never satisfied with what it sees, just are we never satisfied with what we have before us. Or like the ear, which is never satisfied with hearing, so we are never satisfied no matter how much we take in.

Jesus speaks of such a man in Luke 12: 16-21 (ESV). Jesus states, *"And he told them a parable, saying, "The land of a rich man produced plentifully, and he thought to himself, 'What shall I do, for I have nowhere to store my crops?' And he said, 'I will do this: I will tear down my barns and build larger ones, and there I will store all my grain and my goods. And I will say to my soul, 'Soul, you have ample goods laid up for many years; relax, eat, drink, be merry.' But God said to him, 'Fool! This night your soul is required of you, and the things you have prepared, whose will they be?' So is the one who lays up treasure for himself and is not rich toward God."*

The rich man in this story lived beyond his means. As he lived beyond his means he desired more. And his desire for more drove him to obtain more. The reason that he did this is because he believed that he could find peace and satisfaction in all he was working to obtain in this life. All his hard work and effort in chasing what he believed would satisfy him came to a screeching halt in death.

When we look at such stories, we can say that every single human being, to some degree, whether a drug addict, a work addict, a sex addict, or whatever our addiction is, has to realize that we too are like the rich fool. Our desires drive our daily pursuits throughout life and we chase these desires because we believe we can find peace and satisfaction in them. The problem is we are only left feeling hollow and empty once we attain our goals, and ultimately the cycle of pursuit begins all over again.

In the case of drug addicts, every day they wake up and are driven by the anxiety and the fear that their idol has enslaved them into. The fear and panic of how they will achieve their next high is the catalyst for their daily striving after their god. They do everything in their power to get their drug of choice so that they can sacrifice on the altar of their god.

Why does the addict continue to do this? The addict believes their next high will bring them peace and satisfaction. I remember the excitement and the joy I would feel when acquiring more heroin. Not just in the moment when it was in my blood stream, but even on the drive to purchase it. I would feel like I was on cloud nine when my dealer would pull up. And as the heroin entered my hand, before it ever entered my system, I felt extreme satisfaction, comfort, and peace. It was almost like I was already high.

Then, for a brief moment, as the drug entered my bloodstream, I would feel a release of tension. But the thing is this, as quickly as the excitement came, it faded. And the reality of the next day's offering of worship that needed to be made began to loom in the back of my mind. I would seek satisfaction and I would seek peace on a daily basis through heroin but never found it. And the more I was left disappointed by the drug, the more I sought it to solve my problem.

The end result for all addicts, whether they be addicted to drugs, money, sex (you name it) – the end result is that we could die striving for a peace that will never be found in all of our hard work, chasing after something that is worthless. Our idols turn our lives into a rat race in which we chase our own tails in circles day after day, month after month, year after year. We chase our own tails all the way down into our own graves – and then we are dead and it is too late.

9

---•---

What's the Point of Living?

Someone might rightly ask, *"If all of life is a worthless pursuit over things that will never satisfy us then what is the point of living? "* If life is really just a rat race in which we seek to obtain things that will never satisfy or quench our souls, then why live it? Why continue chasing our tails down into our own graves? Why continue going in circles over and over again?

In order to answer this question and understand our condition, we must understand why God created us in the first place. We need to understand the scriptural answer for man's existence.

If we look at Revelation 4:11 (ESV), it reads, *"Worthy are you, our Lord and God, to receive glory and honor and power, for you created all things, and by your will they existed and were created."* The picture painted here is of God sitting on His throne. Surrounding him are heavenly creatures and elders, and they are worshipping Him. God's creatures are singing to Him in worship. What they are saying is that God is worthy of glory, honor, and praise on the basis of who He is and that He is the creator of all things. By Him, everything exists, and thus the creature that He has created owes Him the worship that He is worthy of.

We can see the same truth in Romans 11:36 (ESV). This verse reads, *"For from him and through him and to him are all things. To him be glory forever. Amen."* What this is saying is that all things come through God and all things came by God. All things are for God. Therefore, God deserves glory from all things He created.

Colossians 1:16 (ESV) says, *"For by him all things were created, in heaven and on earth, visible and invisible, whether thrones or dominions or rulers or authorities—all things were created through him and for him."* Through God, all things were created. This includes spiritual things, physical things, government systems, the universe, and the earth – literally everything.

"Our separation from God"

Everything in existence was created by God, and created for God. And all the things created by Him and for Him were created for the purpose that He would be glorified through them. This means that if you and I are God's creation, then we are specifically created to bring Him glory and this is done through our worship of Him. He intricately designed and hardwired us for the purpose of worshiping Him. It is in our nature to worship and it is the basis of our existence.

Our need to worship, however, creates problem in this broken world. We read in Genesis Chapters One, Two and Three about how God intended for His creation to exist in service and worship to Him. We see Adam in the Garden of Eden, walking in fellowship with God. But we also see God setting a standard of righteousness in that garden. God gave the command that if Adam were to eat from the tree of the knowledge of good and evil, Adam would die.

In Genesis 3, we read that Adam did violate God's law and immediately the relationship Adam and Eve had with God changed. The man and woman felt shame from their sinful rebellion against God. They experienced fear. They no longer desired to be in the presence of God. Adam and Eve even lashed out at God and blamed Him for their willing disobedience to His law.

John 1:3-4 states, *"Through Him all things were made, and without Him nothing was made that has been made. In Him was life, and that life was the light of men."* What happened is that Adam and Eve's violation of God's law severed their spiritual relationship with God. In the moment that they sinned, they were severed from the life of God which resulted in spiritual death beginning. According to Romans 5:12, all men have inherited spiritual death from Adam. All descendants of Adam die physically, at the end of their lives, but they're born spiritually dead at the beginning of life.

Spiritual death can best be described as complete severance and separation from God. It is clearly pictured in Isaiah 59:2 (ESV). This passage reads, "*But your iniquities have made a separation between you and your God, and your sins have hidden his face from you so that he does not hear*." Our sin has caused a complete separation between us and God. Our sin even means in our natural state we're completely unwilling to seek Him. We don't even have a natural desire to seek God or genuinely cry out to Him. And even if we did cry out, our sin is such an offense to God that He has turned away from us, so that He wouldn't hear our cries.

Picture two mountains. On one mountain stands mankind and on the other mountain stands God. In between the two is such an infinitely wide and deep chasm that mankind can never bridge the gap between the mountains. This chasm is a bottomless pit, and if men and women were to try and cross it they'd simply fall into utter despair.

This is a picture of our separation from God. Mankind is on one side, God on the other, and sin is between the two. However, this imagery is not the complete picture of sins effect on our relationship with God. Romans 5:10 says that because of sin we're not just separated from God, we're actually enemies of God.

The separation human beings experience through sin also affects the way we as humans behave. Roman 3:10-18 states that no human being is right in God's eyes. It also says that no one can understand the things of God. No one, in and of themselves, truly seeks after God. Every single human being, existing in their natural sinful state of being, actually turns away from God. Our mouths are full of evil and our actions are plagued by violence. We have no reverence for God whatsoever.

Isaiah 64:6-7 reveals that we are all unclean before God in our natural existence. And even our supposedly "good works," when performed as sinful men and women, separated from God, are filthy before Him. It is as if our sin has swept us off our feet. Nothing about God is desirable to us and we melt in the hand of our wickedness. In our sinful condition, we actually love sin. We desire it. Genesis 6:5 says that men's hearts are completely filled with evil all the time. We possess an inherently sinful nature within us. It is our natural desire to sin.

Everything we do is now subject to our willingness towards our naturally sinful disposition. Even the things that would be deemed to be good from a worldly standpoint are done with sinful intentions and expression. Though this may be difficult to grasp, if we are doing anything with any intention other than God's glory, it is idolatry and grounded in sin. The bottom line is that from a natural standpoint, our very nature and being is inclined towards sin and there is absolutely nothing that we can do about it.

So why all this talk about sin? What does sin have to do with addiction?

10

The Problem

What does sin have to do with drug addiction? What does the fact that God created us to worship Him, but that now we're separated from Him, have to do with anyone's addiction to drugs (or anything else)? Looking back at what we've said thus far about addiction, we can see that addiction itself is merely a symptom of a much larger problem. The heart of addiction is idolatry.

When we give ourselves over to idols we are offering ourselves to the demons behind them, and this enslaves us to the control of those demonic forces. And now, looking back at what we've discussed about the human condition, we know that God created man and the inclination to worship is hardwired into human beings. The worship and glory of God is the chief purpose of man. It is the whole reason that we exist, and it is the sole purpose of all of creation. However, the entrance of sin into humanity has now distorted our intended purpose in life by separating us from the only object of worship that will satisfy our souls.

However, this doesn't change the reality that we are still hardwired to worship. In our natural fallen state, our desires now lead us to try to fulfill our purpose in worshiping things in the creation rather than the Creator (Romans 1: 25). Ultimately, such worship never satisfies and only leaves us thirsting for more.

"A counterfeit god"

Jeremiah 17:9 (ESV) says, *"The heart is deceitful above all things, and desperately sick"*. Our sin and separation from God, and the desire to worship, embedded within us, causes our heart to try to fill the void within us that only God can fill. Thus, we start making false gods to worship. Addicts, in their natural inclination to worship, fashion the substance of their choosing into an object of worship that they hope will give them the satisfaction that only God can give!

Addicts hope to find what has left their hearts so hollow in their drugs. The drug an addict chooses to worship is really a counterfeit god. It is used to fill the void in their heart left by sin, which now separates them from God. And in the same way a castaway adrift at sea cannot drink salt water to quench their thirst (because it will eventually kill them), the addict chooses to take their drug of choice in order to try and quench their spiritual thirst (even though that drug will eventually kill them). The more they take in, the more parched they become physically, mentally, and spiritually.

When we worship a drug in an attempt to fill the void that is left in our soul that only God can fill, it does greater damage than just ruining a physical life. It causes the addict to rot spiritually also. Like a dead body that has been laid in the ground, so is the soul of a man who is spiritually dead.

At first the corpse is recognizable, but as time goes on death consumes the flesh and causes it to decay and rot. Romans 1:18-32 gives a picture of human beings in their natural state towards God. This passage says all people know God exists. All people see His creation. When can all look at the stars and the sun and the moon and the wind and see God's handiwork. And yet, instead of inspiring us to worship God, as it should, we instead decide to worship the creation itself. We determine, on our own, what we will decide to worship and what is worthy of our worship.

We trade the glory of God for inanimate objects like heroin, and cocaine, and meth, and money, and sex, and relationships and jobs. We trade the glory of God for things that will never satisfy our souls. Drug addicts take the glory that God deserves and instead embrace something that has no value whatsoever in light of eternity.

The more that we all, as addicts, do this, the more our minds become darkened and our hearts become hardened towards God. The more we reject the one true God, the more we will ourselves over to the worship of demons. And the more we will ourselves over to demonic idols, the more that our minds decay and rot.

This explains the downward spiral most addicts experience as they go deeper and deeper into drug abuse. When first using the drug, the addict finds that it stimulates them in a positive manner, which causes them to come back for that same effect again. One major example of this is found in males who use opioids for the effect that it has on their sexual stamina. However, the more they use it, the deeper and deeper they get, until it begins to consume everything in their life. Men on opioids will use it recreationally during sex and the effect of the drug on their performance boosts their confidence, mental prowess, and decreases any insecurities that they may have in that area.

Yet, with each usage, the desire for the drug transcends social usage and begins to become a necessity for daily functioning. With each day's pursuit and capture of the drug, it becomes higher on the platform of worship, while other priorities fall to the wayside. Each day spent in addiction, this worship causes the mind to grow darker and the heart to grow harder and the soul to decay faster. The longer this goes on the long this goes on the closer they get to the point where the things they once held as important or morally acceptable no longer matter.

It is here where they get to the place where raising their children, and loving them, while once a priority, is no longer at the top of the list of things to do. It is here where sex becomes a tool to be used. It is here where violence becomes a ritualistic pre-requisite to idol worship. It is here that God gives them over to their idols as they proclaim, "*This is what I want to worship…*

This is what I desire to worship... This is my god!" And God lets them have it.

As Romans 1 further explains, the progressive decay of the human mind in idolatry ultimately manifests itself through physical action. This is especially seen manifested through sex, our most carnal desire. As sinful men and women give their hearts and minds over to idols in worship, there is often a physical expression of their spiritual decay seen in their sex lives. This is especially evident in the worship of drugs. Heroin usage commonly goes hand and hand with a moral decay of the sex lives of those using the drug. This can be seen, not only through prostitution, but also in an overall loss of conviction and standard in the individual as to what they personally deem to be sexually acceptable. Both women and men alike lose their sense of independence and personal value, ultimately becoming objects of sexual abuse and manipulation. Just like drug abuse, this is merely the external expression of the core issue of idolatry.

Sexual decay is not the only external expression of idolatry. Rather, spiritual decay spreads to all aspects of the addict's existence and manifests itself through a slew of vile and obscene behaviors. As the drug produces these negative behaviors, they become conditioned to these expressions and begin to utilize them to obtain the drug. The decay that often takes place within the moral fiber of an addict's mind is the use of various sins as a means to obtain and partake in the worship of their drug. Addicts frequently become master manipulators and liars. Prostitutes will use sex to gain money for their drug addiction. Teenagers addicted to drugs will lie and steal from their parents. The person who is down at the bottom and has nowhere else to turn may strong-arm people using violence to get what he or she wants.

The bottom line is addicts become inventors of evil. Their object of worship becomes a part of them and spreads death to consume their entire being. What may have once been viewed as deplorable and heinous before addiction has now become the method of their worship. As the addict submits to the wooing of the drug, the demons behind it tighten their grip around the rotting soul of those trapped in bondage and there is no way to escape its grip.

11

Asking the Question: What's the Answer?

There is absolutely no doubt that the suffering that results from drug addiction is a terrible thing. There is no question about that. I would never be so insensitive as to downplay the personal horror of any individual who is addicted to drugs or alcohol. It is wholly destructive in every way and there is nothing about it that should be taken lightly. However, with all that being said, the individual suffering of the addict is not the worst case scenario. While this may seem like an uncaring statement, the bottom line is – it's the truth.

An example of why an addict's suffering is not the worst case scenario can be found in the effect that heroin has had on my own family. Allow me to introduce you to Amber Masters. Amber was 17 years old. She was absolutely beautiful, excellent in sports and excelled in her school work. Amber was everything her family ever wanted in a daughter and granddaughter. But Amber had a secret that most of the family never knew about. Amber had become addicted to heroin. I didn't find this out until July 17th 2012, when I received a phone call from my father at work telling me that Amber had overdosed and died. It was her grandmother's birthday, and Amber was scheduled to go out with her grandmother to celebrate that very day. But Amber never woke up that morning.

The story that I was told was that the night before she died, Amber went to a recovery meeting where she received heroin from somebody there. That bag of heroin ended up being her last. The next morning the door to her room was locked and her alarm clock was ringing. Her grandparents couldn't get in at first, but when they finally did, they found their granddaughter dead.

Addiction consumes and destroys all it touches. In this circumstance, addiction destroyed the precious future of a bright young woman and permanently left scars of loss in the hearts and minds of everyone who knew her. I can still hear my Uncle Billy (Amber's Pop Pop) saying to me through tears, "Doug, don't put your parents through this!" I can see the effect that Amber's addiction has had on my family many years later. Even as I write this, my heart aches and my eyes are filling with tears as I think about the pain and suffering my loved ones experienced when Amber passed away. Yet, the pain and suffering we feel is not the worst case scenario.

The worst scenario is not homelessness. It's not losing your children. Placing drug addicts in institutions for help isn't the worst thing that can possibly happen to them. Going to prison and losing their freedom is not the end of the road. There is a far worse fate for those who are in addiction as well as mankind in general. This is the same fate that met my beloved cousin Amber on July 17th, 2012. The worst case scenario in addiction is death.

The reality of the matter is that every human being is, at some point, going to die. This is a transcendent truth that will come crashing into the lives of all men and women whether they like it or not. But let's be real. If the Bible isn't true our bodies will go into the ground and just rot. At the point of death, whatever we've worshipped, or given our lives to, will have no bearing on our eternal condition whatsoever. It will not matter because we'll simply cease to exist. We will decay into nothingness and will not have a consciousness of being dead. So if the Bible isn't true, allow me to quote the Apostle Paul who said, we may simply *"eat, drink, and be merry for tomorrow we may die."* (1 Cor. 15:32)

However, if the Bible is true, then what you are about to read is the most important and profound truth you will ever encounter. My prayer and my hope for any addict who might be reading this is that they take heed and listen. The unchangeable reality is that someday you will die. On that day when you breathe your last, you will stand before God and be held accountable for every drug that you made into an idol and every sin that you committed in pursuit of its worship.

On many occasions, I have heard men speak of this day in ignorance. I have heard people say they will stand before God on the day of their death and worry about dealing with Him at that time. Preacher Paul Washer has articulated one of the best responses to this statement that I have ever heard. He stated, "*Did you know this? Death is not natural? Well, death is as natural as birth. No, it is not. Death is supernatural. You don't think God judges men? Hundreds of thousands of men will be swept away into death this very day and most will wake up in hell. Death is not natural. It is supernatural. It is the judgment of God.*"

He describes the judgment of God, "*Imagine a mill stone 10,000 pounds upon the ground and another of like shape and size on top of it and they are hurling and twirling against one another and you take a little grain of wheat and you put it into the middle of them at first for just a microsecond the pressure is felt, the hull is burst, the insides are ground to powder and nothing remains.*"

The final illustration states, "*Just imagine for a moment you are in a little village about an eighth of a mile at the bottom of a huge dam and it is a thousand feet high and a thousand feet wide filled to the brim with water. And you wake up one morning to hear a crack, an explosion like nothing you have ever heard before and as you run to the window and then make your way outside you find that the dam, the wall has been breached. There is nothing left of it. And within a matter of seconds your entire village will be engulfed, the city of destruction. The fleet of foot cannot outrun it. The strongest swimmer will be sucked down. There is no hope.*"

Paul Washer then responds to arrogance of man by stating, "*You say, 'Well, I will stand before God. I will argue my case.' You will melt before God like a tiny wax figurine before a blast furnace.*" (Paul Washer, The Centrality of Christ: http://media.sermonaudio.com/mediapdf/118101012260.pdf)."

This is the reality that awaits each person in death, and at that time there is no one who will stand. Think back to the picture that I used earlier in the book regarding how punishment escalates in severity based on the power and authority of the one who is offended. Honestly examine your life and assess yourself before the law of God, just as I did. Now ask yourself, "*What would happen if I slapped a holy and righteous God in the face? What if I have slapped him hundreds of thousands of times during my entire life?*"

12

The Worst Case Scenario

Let us take a journey into the worst case scenario. Imagine that you, a heroin addict, decide that today is that last day you will ever get high. This is it. No more withdrawal, no more pain, no more fear. Tomorrow, you're going to turn over a new leaf. Tomorrow, you think to yourself, *"I'm going to choose to free myself from it forever!"*

Today, however, is a different story. Imagine you are down to your last few bags and you have to finish them so that you can move towards your new tomorrow. Imagine that you empty those bags into a spoon and then draw them through the cotton into the syringe. Now imagine injecting the contents into your veins. *"This is it,"* you think, *"the last time I am getting high."*

Imagine that you can feel the drug coursing through your blood. You feel the rush of the high accompanied by the peace of partaking in worship. You immediately pull a cigarette out of your pack and light it. As the seconds move past the injection and turn to minutes, your breathing slows. Your face becomes heavy as your eyes roll back into your skull. A frown hangs on your face from the loss of your muscle control. The ash on your cigarette is now longer that the cigarette itself and as all this is happening, you lose consciousness.

Imagine, as you fade into unconsciousness, that your respiratory system begins to fade with you. You have now stopped breathing. Your heart has stopped beating and the blood that carries oxygen to your brain ceases to move. Imagine that your brain begins to drown in fluid and there is absolutely nothing you can do in this moment to jumpstart your heart, pump the blood, or take another breath. Your time has run out, the day has come, and you have now passed from life to death. The Bible speaks of this moment stating, "*And just as it is appointed for man to die once, and after that comes judgment.*" (Heb. 9:27)

"You cannot escape this horror"

Now imagine that you slip into an unconscious state of death and then immediately wake back up. Only you don't wake up at the place where you once were. Instead, imagine you are seated in a courtroom. However, this court room is like no other court room you've ever been in before. What makes this court room so unique is the one who is sitting on the bench. The Judge seated before you is not like human judges – judges who have made erroneous decisions, or who've upheld a flawed standard of right and wrong. This Judge is perfect.

The great Judge is high above you. He's never made a wrong call in His existence. He has never, ever judged wrongly. Furthermore, the law that He upholds is not like imperfect human standards of justice. His standard is perfect and right; it is the exact representation of the Judge's perfect character. The judge's perfection before you gives you a sense and a feeling of guilt that you cannot shake or run from. His presence reveals your guilt before His law and the impending judgment that awaits you before the evidence is ever presented.

Now imagine that you look down at yourself and you are completely naked, with nothing to cover you. You try to cover yourself and hide your shame, but the Judge's gaze pierces through your nakedness and into the depths of your soul. You are completely exposed before the court, in all of your wrongdoing and nothing is hidden from His sight. Now picture that on either side of this judge are countless witnesses, all of whom look intently at your naked exposure.

Picture the courtroom. You are seated at the defense table before the Judge's bench. Across from you is the prosecution's table and on this table is a video projector that begins to roll. It starts by showing the very moment you were born, and it goes all the way until your heart stopped beating and your physical brain ceased to function. What it showed, from your birth to your death, is every single violation of this Judge's law that you have ever committed. This includes all disobedience as a child to every single time you lied, stole or hurt somebody. Every single sin you have ever committed is presented before the Judge as evidence against you.

Now let's take things a step deeper. Imagine the projector not only shows every single sinful action that you've ever committed, but every single sinful thought and desire you've ever had. We're talking every single hateful thought you've ever had in your mind about somebody else.

Even worse, every single sexual thought you've ever stored within the depths of your soul is presented before the Judge. You know that deep dark secret that you've buried deep within the depths of your subconscious? The things that you have stored away – the type of secrets that would crush you if anyone else knew about them- are all presented before the Judge. Imagine that who you are on the inside, behind all the masks and facades, was revealed before God. In that moment – everything is uncovered.

By the time the projector stops rolling, your undeniable guilt has been so firmly established in front of the judge that you begin weeping uncontrollably. The weight of what you have done bears upon you in such a way that you feel you cannot breath. You try to catch your breath through the tears, but there is nothing you can do but weep. You scream and plead aloud to anyone who will listen for mercy, but the time for mercy has expired.

In the midst of your sorrow the Judge stands at the bench and speaks directly to you. His voice pierces through you like a knife in your heart and He asks, "Is there anything you can say to justify yourself?" What can be said about all of the drugs you worshipped as an idol? What will save you from punishment for all the vile things you did in your addiction? How will you try to explain your worship of idols? There is, of course, nothing you can say to save yourself from justice. The Judge swings down the gavel and declares you to be guilty. And at that moment, guards enter the court room and place shackles on your hands and feet, and they escort you out the court room.

The Bible compares our judgement to a lake of fire. It also compares it to being cast into a terrible darkness. Mark 9:42 (ESV) says *"Whoever causes one of these little ones who believe in me to sin, it would be better for him if a great millstone were hung around his neck and he were thrown into the sea."*

Think of being in God's heavenly court, your hands and feet shackled, being walked out by the guards. Immediately upon exiting the court room, imagine you are standing on a dock in the middle of the night.

This dock goes out over a lake filled with raging waters. Imagine that the guards walk you to the edge of the lake and place a steel bracelet around your neck and attached to this bracelet is a chain. This chain is then attached to a boulder that is infinitely heavier than anything you could ever lift. As the guards walk you and this massive weight to the edge of the dock you begin to understand what they are about to do. Sheer terror overtakes you as you begin pleading with them not to push the boulder into the water. You grab their clothes and scream and beg, *"Please don't push me into the water!"* But there is no going back. They stare at you with indignation as one who has slapped the Most Holy in the face. You try to free yourself from the chain, but you cannot. There is nothing to stop the inevitable from happening. The guards push the boulder into the black water.

You begin grabbing at the chain with all your might, hoping to stop the slack from running out. You scream for help, but no one hears. All of your efforts, strength, and work amounts to nothing as you try to halt your impending doom. In a matter of seconds the slack runs out.

Now you're pulled headfirst into the water. You try to scratch and claw your way back up to the surface, but you cannot. The harder you fight, the quicker your oxygen depletes. You are dragged deeper and deeper into the abyss. You look up and see the moon above appear smaller and smaller, until there is nothing left around you except total darkness. You are now consumed in utter blackness.

Imagine that 30 seconds goes by … then 45 seconds … and then 60 seconds. At a minute and a half the pressure on your chest causes your lungs to feel as though they are going to explode. The deeper you fall into the depths, the more intense the feeling of drowning is to the point that you feel as though your whole body is being crushed. In less than two minutes, you make the decision that you would rather die than to suffer such agony. You make the choice to breathe in and accept your fate. The problem is… death has already come and this is your eternal state now. There will be nothing but endless time to continue experiencing the horror of being in this utter darkness. And the first 1000 years you are there in the water of God's judgment is like those first seconds after you were dropped into it.

This is the cup of God's wrath upon the sinner for their transgression of the law. The reality is that justice must always be satisfied. All who are guilty of sin must be punished.

"What if this happened instead?"

Now place yourself back in the same courtroom. Imagine the Judge has just asked, *"Is there anything that you can say to justify yourself?"* The guards come and place the shackles on your wrists and feet. The Judge stands up to swing his gavel down and declare you guilty. Yet before you are declared guilty, a man walks into the courtroom. As this man walks past you, he smiles. You have no idea who this man is – but He knows you. This man walks directly past you to the Judge with an authority that you could never have because of your guilt before the law.

The man walks up to the judge and says *"Your honor, my Father, this man, this woman deserves every single thing that they receive for their violation of your law. But, your Honor, before the foundation of the world, I have determined that I will take their place and I will be judged on their behalf that they may not have to drink the cup of your anger and wrath."*

1 John 2:1-2 (ESV) says *"My little children, I am writing these things to you so that you may not sin. But if anyone does sin, we have an advocate with the Father, Jesus Christ the righteous. He is the propitiation for our sins, and not for ours only but also for the sins of the whole world."*

Imagine now that when the man says those words and offers Himself up before the courts of the Judge on your behalf, the guards take the shackles off you. In that moment, the Judge points to the man and declares him guilty on your behalf. The guards then walk over to the man. They beat Him mercilessly and then they nail Him to a cross. And every drop of His blood is shed to pay the debt that you accrued by your transgressions against the law.

When the man finally dies on that cross, his death serves to satisfy the sentence that you deserved to serve. Every bit of God's anger is satisfied by this man, as every drop of his blood on the cross serves to satisfy the wrath of God that should have been placed upon you instead.

Imagine if you will that this man willingly walked out of the courtroom straight to the edge of the dock. Picture him taking that boulder – which is the weight of the guilt and shame you accrued by your sin – picking it up, placing it on his own back and willingly jumping into the waters of God's judgment. And now, he sinks into the depths of God's anger and wrath towards your sin. Imagine that he took the justice that you deserved.

The good news is that he sank to the bottom of that lake of judgment and began to drink every drop of God's anger towards you until the lake was dry! And when the last drop was gone and God's wrath was satisfied, he broke the chains that sin had put on him and walked out of the lake.

It is at the point where the wrath of God against you has been totally removed, and the man on the cross breaks free from the death he has suffered on your behalf. He becomes alive once again and walks back into the courtroom and declares that you are now innocent of the charges that were once brought against you. He declares you innocent of all your idolatry, addiction, lies, cheating, and every sin you have ever committed. Through his victory, your shame has been covered and your sin has been conquered! This is the truth of what Jesus has done for us on the cross. And it is by this truth that we can find true freedom from every kind of sin, including sins of addiction.

13

How Does Jesus Dying on the Cross Free Me from Addiction?

How does Jesus dying on the cross free an addict from addiction? The truth is that there is no "practical methodology" that can be given with regards to freedom from addiction by the blood of Jesus. There is no simple five-step program to success.

There is no program of simple prayers that can be said that result in anyone, all the sudden, being freed from their addiction. Nor is there any type of "ninety meetings in ninety days" system that guarantees cure. No magic drug will free anyone and neither will secular programs. As Christian rapper Timothy Brindle says, *"Our help is not in 12 Steps, or in books on the shelf that sells best, like health and wealth mess that compels self's flesh. Cause with self-help, guess what? You're helpless! (Lyrics by Timothy Brindle, from "The All-Sufficiency of Christ", Lamp Mode Recordings)"*

The problem is that programs, sinner's prayers, 12-step programs, etc., all rely on an addict playing some part in their own deliverance. When we bring anything to the table in regard to our salvation, we are sharing the spotlight with the only One who deserves worship. Since God has created us to worship Him alone, He must be the only hero in the story. Anything else that shares the spotlight with Him is just another idol that we have fashioned, even if that idol is us worshiping ourselves.

"The heart of the addict"

If we were created to worship God and that is the chief goal and purpose of mankind, then all glory must go to Him. True salvation is an act of His doing alone, with us bringing nothing to the table.

As I say this, someone might well ask, *"What about all those people who get off drugs apart from Jesus?"* This is a valid observation and an appropriate question. If my primary intention in creating this book is to help people get off drugs then my argument here will absolutely fail.

There are many people who do eventually get off drugs, apart from Jesus. What happens, however, is that their worship merely shifts from drugs to something else, such as work, a human relationship, the program they participate in, or some other idol that they fashion.

I am most certainly a prime example of a person who would have times of sobriety by shifting my worship to idols other than drugs. This explains why I stopped doing heroin as I began worshiping my ex-girlfriend. You see, I have a philosophy regarding getting off drugs apart from Christ that says the devil, Satan, doesn't really care what you glorify and worship so long as it's not the one true God. Please take a moment and let that sink in.

The real goal of this writing is to help people go beyond getting off drugs and go to the core of the problem. To help them move beyond the symptom and address the root cause, which is our fallen sinful nature. My true hope and desire is that in accepting the message of the gospel, you may be reconciled to God. In reconciliation to Him, you may finally find that which can satisfy your soul and fulfill your purpose in life through worshiping Him – something that no idol, including drugs, can ever do.

How does Jesus' work on the cross cure the heart of a drug addict? If we look at 2 Corinthians 5:16-21 (ESV) we read, *"From now on, therefore, we regard no one according to the flesh. Even though we once regarded Christ according to the flesh, we regard him thus no longer. Therefore, if anyone is in Christ, he is a new creation. The old has passed away; behold, the new has come. All this is from God, who through Christ reconciled us to himself and gave us the ministry of reconciliation; that is, in Christ God was reconciling the world to himself, not counting their trespasses against them, and entrusting to us the message of reconciliation. Therefore, we are ambassadors for Christ, God making his appeal through us. We implore you on behalf of Christ, be reconciled to God. For our sake he made him to be sin who knew no sin, so that in him we might become the righteousness of God.*"

What we must begin to understand is what all of us, including the addict, is really in need of. What we need is our separation with God to end and our reconciliation with God to be established. Since the purpose of every human being, including the drug addict, is to worship God, that purpose needs to be restored! In order for a person's relationship with God to be restored, their sin needs to be taken away in Christ.

How is sin removed from anyone? 2 Corinthians 5:21 (ESV) states *"For our sake he made him to be sin who knew no sin, so that in him we might become the righteousness of God."* An astounding thing took place in the life of Jesus that culminated on the cross.

In His love for His people, God entered into His fallen creation and took on the form of human flesh, becoming truly human. He then lived under the same laws that we have broken. Yet, unlike our forefather Adam, Jesus (the God-man) was perfect in all His faith and was perfect in His relationship with God. Because of this, He did not deserve to experience death.

But if the wages of sin are death then why did Jesus die? According to2 Corinthians 5:21, God the Father took our sin and placed it on Jesus. When Jesus was nailed to that cross, our sin was nailed with Him. When Jesus hung on that cross, our sin hung with Him.

We know this because in Matthew 27:46 He cries, *"My God, my God, why have you forsaken me?"* The Father turned away from the Son because sin separates man from God and His innocent Son had taken our sin upon Himself. So when Jesus died on that cross, our sin died with Him. When He entered His grave, our sin entered with Him. All of God's anger and punishment for every sin we've ever committed was poured out on Jesus. God's anger, wrath, and justice were all satisfied in Jesus, who took what we deserved on our behalf.

We are separated from God by our sins: past, present, and future. Yet Jesus has paid the debt for our sins: past, present, and future. Jesus died and took the punishment for every drug and idol we've ever worshipped. Colossians 2:14 (ESV) says that Jesus *"By canceling the record of debt that stood against us with its legal demands. This He set aside, nailing it to the cross."* Jesus took our debt, which separated us from God. He took our idols. He took our addictions. He took all the things that kept us from fulfilling our purpose in this life, by worshipping the one true God, and He nailed them to the cross.

And Jesus not only did that, He took His righteousness that He had by keeping the entire law, and He places it upon those He saves. When God now looks upon an addict who is saved, He doesn't see a sinful person who is a slave to their desires any longer. He doesn't see the addict who didn't raise their children. He doesn't see the addict who worshipped the drugs. He sees His Son, who is perfect and blameless, instead. If our sin is removed from us, and it has been judged, then what we have to realize is that the separation between us and God has been removed as well. We can be reconciled to Him. In Jesus and His work on the cross, we can fulfill the reason that we were created in the first place. We were created to worship and through Christ we can now rightfully worship the one true God.

14

Once an Addict, Always an Addict?

Looking back at what Jesus did on the cross for us, we can be sure that addiction is one of the many sins that were nailed to the cross with Him. When Jesus died, every sort of addiction died with Jesus. When Jesus was laid in the tomb, every kind of addiction was laid in the tomb with Him. Jesus paid the price for all of our sins, including addiction.

The good news for the addict is that he or she is not only united with Christ spiritually through His crucifixion and death, but also in His resurrection! More wonderful news is that when Jesus rose, He left the sin that He bore behind in the grave. Since Jesus rose and left addiction in the grave then an addict who repents of their sin can leave it in that tomb as well.

2 Corinthians 5:17 (ESV) states *"Therefore, if anyone is in Christ, he is a new creation. The old has passed away; behold, the new has come."* An addict's heart, although separated from God and worshipping a drug, and hardened and calloused by sin, can be

changed. Jesus rose and now offers a new heart for addicts. He offers a heart that desires to worship God. He offers a new heart that is able to worship God. Jesus offers us a heart that can grow to love God and move away from sin.

"Who will deliver me from this body of death?"

In Christ, an addict is spiritually made anew. If we are in Jesus we are a new creation. God does all of this so that in our new condition the world may see His mighty work in us, we may know His amazing love, and ultimately so that He is glorified through us.

Many people in this world believe that once someone becomes a drug addict, they will always be an addict. The truth however, is that if one is saved in Jesus then they are truly saved and nothing can reverse or undo what Christ has done. Satan cannot take one's identity or security in Jesus and Satan cannot undo what Jesus has done. Nothing can make God see you as anything but righteous. No addict has to stay in slavery and worship idols. Once an addict belongs to Christ, nothing can take their salvation and escape from addiction away. Once an addict is in Christ, they no longer have to bear the name "addict, " because they are now called sons and daughters of the living God.

As creatures that are hardwired for worship, before Christ we had no choice but to worship idols. We were bound to worship something, but addicts were ultimately unable to worship the only God that can truly satisfy. We were slaves to sin and in complete bondage to our idols. However, the good news comes in Romans 6:5-11, which states, *"For if we have been united with him in a death like his, we shall certainly be united with him in a resurrection like his. We know that our old self was crucified with him in order that the body of sin might be brought to nothing, so that we would no longer be enslaved to sin.* [7] *For one who has died has been set free from sin. Now if we have died with Christ, we believe that we will also live with him. We know that Christ, being raised from the dead, will never die again; death no longer has dominion over him. For the death he died he died to sin, once for all, but the life he lives he lives to God. So you also must consider yourselves dead to sin and alive to God in Christ Jesus."*

In our union with Jesus' and his work on the cross, we are set free from the bondage and slavery of sin that had mastered us. Now, we are reunited and reconciled to the only Master worthy of all praise, honor, and glory. In Jesus' work alone, we are able to worship God and focus on fulfilling our purpose in life. In Christ, we are new people, with a new purpose, and a new reason for living!

The problem then becomes that Satan seeks to keep an addict focused on the person they once were, rather than on the new person they can become in Jesus. There is no reason for an addict who becomes a Christian to feel guilty over sins that Christ died for already. This is why it's important for all Christians to understand we cannot fundamentally change our lives through the power of our own efforts.

If we attempt do this, Satan will mock us when we fail. He will even try to make us question our own salvation in Christ on the basis of our inability to live perfectly. Even after someone becomes a Christian they will still struggle and wrestle with sin. Until we die, we will still live in a body and in a world that is subject to sin. We will fight battles against sin until the day we die.

Even the one who is often considered the greatest apostle of all, the Apostle Paul, struggled and fought against sin. Paul writes, *"For we know that the law is spiritual, but I am of the flesh, sold under sin. For I do not understand my own actions. For I do not do what I want, but I do the very thing I hate. Now if I do what I do not want, I agree with the law, that it is good. So now it is no longer I who do it, but sin that dwells within me. For I know that nothing good dwells in me, that is, in my flesh. For I have the desire to do what is right, but not the ability to carry it out. For I do not do the good I want, but the evil I do not want is what I keep on doing. Now if I do what I do not want, it is no longer I who do it, but sin that dwells within me. So I find it to be a law that when I want to do right, evil lies close at hand. For I delight in the law of God, in my inner being, but I see in my members another law waging war against the law of my mind and making me captive to the law of sin that dwells in my members. Wretched man that I am! Who will deliver me from this body of death?"* (Romans 7:14-25)

Even though he had acquired a new nature in Christ, even though he loved God and desired to worship God through obedience, his flesh still tried to draw him back to his old ways. Paul was still tempted to do things he didn't want to do, and he often didn't do the good things he did want to do. What we have to realize is that if the Apostle Paul struggled with this internal war then we're definitely going to struggle also.

An example of this would be how even Christian men often struggle with lust. Even though I am married, if a pretty woman walks by, I often feel temptation to give her a second glance. I fight against this, and the more I do the more I am reminded that I am in the same position as the Apostle Paul. *"Wretched man that I am! Who will deliver me from this body of death?"* I certainly cannot deliver myself!

Paul's conclusion in this matter, in verse 25, is the truth. It has truly helped to free me from the guilt and shame that I feel when I fall into temptation. Paul's conclusion is this: *"Wretched man that I am! Who will deliver me from this body of death? Thanks be to God through Jesus Christ our Lord!"*

Coming out of my addiction, I would struggle with lust and with a desire to get high. I learned from Paul that, as sin comes and rears its ugly head and I feel that I cannot stop it, the Lord calls us to turn from our sin and look to Jesus. Paul, in the midst of his own struggle against sin, unable to stop, turned from it and fixed his eyes upon Jesus. Paul realized his inability to save himself and he looked to the salvation that God had already provided in Jesus on that cross.

It is in the truth of the fact that our debt has already been paid in Jesus that sin is defeated. Through the work of Jesus we find our strength, our hope, and our courage to push forward. We find this not in ourselves, but in Jesus and Jesus alone, to the glory of God.

Romans 8:1 (ESV) says, *"There is therefore now no condemnation for those who are in Christ Jesus."* There is no condemnation for anyone in Christ, no matter how much they are accused. No matter how much we fail to be perfect according to the law. No matter how much Satan points the finger of accusation at us, there is no condemnation for those who are in Christ Jesus. When we feel temptation, shame, guilt, and accusations being hurled at us for our sin, we don't rely on our ability to fight back, we focus on the fight that Jesus has already won!

If you are in Christ, when Satan points the finger at you and he says, *"You have failed again,"* then you can point to the cross and respond, *"Jesus has succeeded on my behalf."* When Satan points the finger and says, *"You cannot please God,"* you can point to the cross and respond, *"The Father was pleased to crush His Son on my behalf."* When Satan says, *"God will not look past what you've done. He will not look past your addiction. He will not look past all the vial things that you did in worship of your drug,"* you point to the cross and reply, *"He looked upon Christ bearing my sins and judged Him for every single one."*

When Satan says, *"You're still a slave to your addiction,"* you can point to the cross and say, *"Jesus bought my freedom by His blood.*" When Satan says you are guilty then you can point to the cross and say, "*In Christ, God sees me as innocent.*" And when Satan says you are still a junkie, you are still a drug addict, you are still the monster you once were, then you can point to the cross and say, "*I am in Christ and the old me who worshipped the drugs is gone. The old me who loved my sin is dead. Drugs are not my master anymore; I have a new master. He bought me with His own blood and paid my debt in full. The old me was crucified with Him and lies in a grave and a new me has risen in Jesus. And, therefore, I am in Christ. I am a new creation. The old me has passed away. Behold, in Jesus' cross, the new me has come.*"

15

---•---

Is the Juice Worth the Squeeze?

Saying goodbye to the old body of sin within each of us is hard. It is easily the most difficult thing I have ever experienced. It is even harder than going through the actual physical withdrawal from drugs that I went through after my conversion to Christ.

Scripture calls us to put away the old sins, so that the life we once lived dies. This may include saying goodbye to former friends, significant others, places, and hobbies, etc. In addition to the physical and mental pain of withdrawal from addictive substances, God will often call us to walk away from the whole entire world of sin that we have built around us.

In my own circumstance, God called me to lose just about everything and everyone that was a part of my life when I was an addict. I left the girl I was dating and in an addictive, codependent relationship with. I walked away from every single friend that I had who was a part of my former lifestyle, whether an addict or not. I gave up all the former social settings that I once attended. This included any association with bars, concerts, parties and any other settings that promoted the sin I once walked in. I walked away from all of them.

I even stopped listening to music and movies that promoted the type of lifestyle I had lived while pursuing the worship of drugs. This means that on top of all the physical and mental withdrawals that I went through, there was an added pain of heartbreak from losing everything else my world was built upon. Virtually everything that I was familiar with and that I loved came to an end. This caused certain people to become angry with me. My former friends hated me. I was mocked in my old social scene. It all hurt badly.

"Conviction drives a true Christian to repentance"

Jesus, however, paints an extreme picture of how to deal with sin in Mark 9:43-48 (ESV). Jesus says, *"And if your hand causes you to sin, cut it off. It is better for you to enter life crippled than with two hands to go to Hell, to the unquenchable fire. And if your foot causes you to sin, cut it off. It is better for you to enter life lame than with two feet to be thrown into Hell. And if your eye causes you to sin, tear it out. It is better for you to enter the kingdom of God with one eye than with two eyes to be thrown into Hell, 'where their worm does not die and the fire is not quenched.'"*

Jesus paints an extreme picture of how sin needs to be dealt with. He says, *"if your hand causes you to sin, cut it off." "If your foot causes you to sin, cut it off." "If your eye causes you to sin, tear it out.*" Isn't that a bit extreme? Well, to those who have no fear of God, to whom Christ has not opened their eyes to their own sin, the answer is absolutely, "yes."

However, to those who Christ has saved, the answer is an emphatic, "*No.*" The reason believers grow to feel this way is because they come to know and accept the judgement of God. They also know the great love that God has shown his people in removing their sin through Jesus dying on the cross. These truths grow in the heart of the Christian. Removing temptation to sin and turning and walking away from sin is a serious matter. In fact, it's a sign of true and sincere salvation. This is known as repentance.

Ezekiel 36:22-32 says, "*Therefore say to the house of Israel, Thus says the Lord GOD: It is not for your sake, O house of Israel, that I am about to act, but for the sake of my holy name, which you have profaned among the nations to which you came. And I will vindicate the holiness of my great name, which has been profaned among the nations, and which you have profaned among them. And the nations will know that I am the LORD, declares the Lord GOD, when through you I vindicate my holiness before their eyes. I will take you from the nations and gather you from all the countries and bring you into your own land. I will sprinkle clean water on you, and you shall be clean from all your uncleannesses, and from all your idols I will cleanse you. And I will give you a new heart, and a new spirit I will put within you. And I will remove the heart of stone from your flesh and give you a heart of flesh. And I will put my Spirit within you, and cause you to walk in my statutes and be careful to obey my rules. You shall dwell in the land that I gave to your fathers, and you shall be my people, and I will be your God. And I will deliver you from all your uncleannesses. And I will summon the grain and make it abundant and lay no famine upon you. I will make the fruit of the tree and the increase of the field abundant, that you may never again suffer the disgrace of famine among the nations. Then you will remember your evil ways, and your deeds that were not good, and you will loathe yourselves for your iniquities and your abominations. It is not for your sake that I will act, declares the Lord GOD; let that be known to you. Be ashamed and confounded for your ways, O house of Israel."*

What we're seeing here in Ezekiel is God promising salvation to His people. He promises that He is going to wash them clean. He is going to give them a new heart. He is going to place a new spirit within them. After God washes His people's sins away and He places the new nature in them, He states that He will cause them to walk in His statutes and obey His rules. For His people to do otherwise would be contrary to their new nature.

In 2 Corinthians 7:10 we read, *"For godly grief produces a repentance that leads to salvation without regret, whereas worldly grief produces death."* Before, when we sinned, our nature and flesh were in agreement with another so sin felt desirable and natural. When we are separated from God but our heart desires to worship, we try to fill that void with drugs, with alcohol, with sex, with money, with whatever it is that we are

113

worshipping. Our pursuit of it feels desirable and it feels natural to us. We enjoy it. We like it.

After someone comes to Christ, however, and that Christian begins to mature in faith, their new nature and the old flesh stand in opposition to one another. When we then do things in our flesh that are contrary to the nature Christ has placed within us, a tug-of-war begins. And sin, as we grow in Him, begins to feel unnatural. It begins to produce a godly sorrow within us. And this conviction drives a true Christian to repentance. This is a sign that salvation has really taken place.

As we mature, the same moral law that once condemned a person will now be the desire of a Christian's heart. A true Christian no longer sees God's law as something that places them under condemnation, but as something that they desire and want. Jesus said in John 14:15 (ESV), "*If you love me, you will keep my commandments.*" A sign of genuine Christian salvation is a love for Jesus and for what He's done for us, and this means we will also desire to obey Him at any cost.

Looking back now at Mark 9:43-48, we can see this passage isn't talking about doing things to avoid Hell. Those who are in Christ have already been delivered from Hell by Jesus' sacrifice on the cross. A true confirmation of this in a Christian's life is their desire to grow in the grace of what Christ has done for them, which it turn causes them to not want to continue to sin.

It means that, as a Christian, I am willing to cut off anything in my life that causes me to sin. I'd be willing to lose a hand or a foot, metaphorically speaking, if they cause me to disobey Christ. As Christians, as we grow in Him, we are willing to give over everything that leads us to sin. Not because we are obligated to, but because we love Him and want to.

Practically, this is a picture of long-term suffering versus short-term pleasure, as compared to short-term suffering versus long-term pleasure. The short-term pleasure would be an addict continuing in their addiction. They would get the immediate satisfaction of keeping their sinful lifestyle and everything that comes with it. But such things will bring long-term suffering, all the way into eternity.

Compared to what Jesus is saying, it's better to suffer short-term, by cutting off the eyes, hands and feet of sin. When a Christian cuts off the things in their life that leads them to sin then the suffering is only for a brief time in their life, but there are wonderful, everlasting ramifications that come from it.

When it came to my own drug addiction, I walked with Christ and suffered for a short time during the period of giving them up entirely. Christ's work in me caused me to turn from all the sins that contributed to my addiction. As I grew to understand what He had done on that cross for me, He gave me the strength to cut out the evil influences in my life that related to drugs.

Christ gave me the strength to pluck out old places and sever things that had contributed to my idolatry and addiction instead of allowing me to cling to my idols and suffer for an eternity in Hell.

When I worshiped God in Christ and sought Him, I naturally began to shift away from the old desires that encouraged drug abuse. As I fixed my eyes on Him, it made sobriety come easier, as all of the former things that triggered my addiction were removed.

Friends who used or encouraged me to get high were gone. The places and situations that promoted my usage were removed. Any forms of entertainment that promoted my usage were cut off. As I turned toward obedience to Jesus, I was simultaneously turning from using drugs and addiction altogether without even realizing it.

In my personal experience, nothing about this is ever easy and it hurts. However, as I grow in faith and I learn the depths of what Jesus did for me, there is no social setting that I am not willing to give up, if necessary, for Christ. There is no earthly friend that is worth more than what Jesus paid to buy me from sin and death. There is nothing that is worth more than what Jesus paid on that cross. As I still grow and am learning to understand this, deeper and deeper, I desire Him more and more.

This understanding of how a Christian is called to deal with sin doesn't come about immediately. But rather, as a believer begins growing in Him, this is something God brings to a believer's understanding and conscience overtime. Throughout the course of their life, God begins to deal with a believer about certain sins, little bit by little bit.

Certainly this is not a one size fits all experience. Some people mature faster than others, while others may mature slower than others. God also works on different areas of peoples' lives in different ways and at different times. This maturing, just like salvation, is a work of God alone so that we cannot boast in any of our growth. But we can boast of Him for the good work that he is doing in us.

As you read this book, as you look at these things, you have to ask the question, "*Is the juice worth the squeeze?*" Are you willing, in pursuit of Jesus, to give up everything that leads you to sin? Are you willing to give up drugs, not so that you can simply have sobriety, but so that you can have Him?

Conclusion

---•---

What Do You Believe?

With everything that has been said up to this point, we might now ask, *"What do you believe?"* Do you believe that you, on your own, have the strength to overcome addiction? If so, then how come you haven't overcome it yet? How come every stretch of sobriety is centered on supplementing your addiction with a new god to worship?

Honestly assess yourself. How many times have you gotten sober by entering into a new relationship only for that relationship to fall apart and you returning to drugs? How many times have programs caused you to gain short-term sobriety and you put your faith in your ability to work the program, only to fail and relapse? We all know people who have put all their eggs into the basket of recovery programs and their ability to work the steps unto temporal salvation. Yet, one day everything collapses and all that work amounts to nothing in a moment of weakness. Or what about those who fall in love and decide that they will leave drugs behind forever. This is, of course, until the relationship fails and they have nothing to grasp a hold of and they inevitably return to the altar of the drug.

The circumstances vary from person to person, but the story is the same.

Maybe you associate yourself with some particular social circle. Perhaps you find your identity in your sexuality or in music. Perhaps you find your identity in a certain clique or a group of people, only for that group of people – that identity that you formed for yourself – to fail you. Then you return to drugs. Did you feel just as hollow in your latest identity as you did in your previous one? How many times have you supplemented your worship of a drug with the worship of something else?

"A beautiful place to be"

If the end game in your battle with addiction is to simply stop using drugs and you have done so, congratulations on your success. Whether you would like to admit it or not, though the symptoms have been masked, under the surface the condition remains the same. That same void that drove you to drugs still exists and it will never be filled as long as you rely on anything within your own ability to fill it. As long as your strength and ability play a part in quenching your soul's thirst, you will remain thirsty. You will strive to find peace in your life and you will continue to chase this all the way into your grave. Do you rely on yourself for success or has the will to keep fighting been utterly broken out of you?

Have you come to a place of such brokenness that you have nothing left? Is the weight of sin drowning

119

you in the depths of your addiction? Is the fight over? Do you have nothing left? Does Ephesians 2:1-3 (ESV) describe you when it says, *"And you were dead in the trespasses and sins in which you once walked, following the course of this world, following the prince of the power of the air, the spirit that is now at work in the sons of disobedience— among whom we all once lived in the passions of our flesh, carrying out the desires of the body and the mind, and were by nature children of wrath, like the rest of mankind?"*

Do you realize that you are spiritually dead? Have you been given over to the seduction of this world? Are you controlled by demonic influence to use drugs? Are you consumed by your mind and your body and desire to worship your drug as a god? Do you fear that when you die you will stand before Him and be held accountable for this sin?

If that is where you are then what a beautiful place to be.   I vividly remember this place of hopeless abandonment. Not hopeless abandonment in God, but hopeless abandonment of myself. That place of such brokenness where I knew that I had nothing left to offer. That place where I laid down all of my efforts and trying. Oh what a beautiful place this is for you!

This place of brokenness finds its beauty in the words of the Apostle Paul, when he finishes his thought in Ephesians 2:4-9 (ESV), which states, *"But God, being rich in mercy, because of the great love with which he loved us, even when we were dead in our trespasses, made us alive together with Christ—by grace you have been saved—and raised us up with him and seated us with him in the heavenly places in Christ Jesus, so that in the coming ages he might show the immeasurable riches of his grace in kindness toward us in Christ Jesus. For by grace you have been saved through faith. And this is not your own doing; it is the gift of God, not a result of works, so that no one may boast."*

When it says, *"But God,"* that God, in verse 4, is the counteractive measure to your addiction. *"But God,"* shows you that in the midst of our spiritual death God will come to you, and unite you with Christ, not only in His death but also in His resurrection! God will freely give you grace through the work of Jesus on the cross. And this grace will be given to you on the basis of nothing that you have done. None of your effort will contribute to it. It is all of His doing, in His love for you, to the praise of His wonderful name!

Do you believe this? If you believe this then your faith is confirmation that God has applied His grace to you. Paul proclaims this wonderful news by stating, *"For by grace you have been saved through faith. And this is not your own doing; it is the gift of God, not a result of works, so that no one may boast* (Eph. 2:8-9)."

What this is saying is that your faith is a gift of God produced by the grace He has given you in Jesus. If you truly believe that you bring nothing to the table and your works are of no value in the equation. If you fall helplessly at the mercy of God, through the work of the cross for your salvation, then your faith is a confirmation that God will declare you righteous through Jesus' sacrifice upon cross on your behalf. You no longer have to worship the drug because you are free to worship the Lord. You will finally be able to worship the way you were created to worship. In Jesus, you can now be reconciled to God. You can drink and your thirst will be quenched.

About the Author...

Douglas Clarke (B.S., M.A.) is currently the Aftercare Manager of Jubilee Ministries in Lebanon, Pennsylvania. Prior to this, Douglas was the Operations Manager of Luzerne Treatment Center and the Facility Director of GEO Group's Broad Street Re-entry Facility. Currently, Douglas is working on his second Master's Degree (M.Div.) at Westminster Theological Seminary. Douglas is married to his wife, Lindsay, and they have three children, Anthony, Chloe, and Ezekiel.

For more information about Doug and his work, visit **www.FreedomFromSubstances.com**

Made in the USA
Columbia, SC
06 October 2020